NOTHING BEETS
BORSCHT

Jane Blanksteen

NOTHING BEETS BORSCHT

Jane's Russian Cookbook

ATHENEUM · NEW YORK

1974

DRAWINGS BY IRENE RUTENBERG

The material on pages 221 and 222 is based on a recipe in *Lessons in Gourmet Cooking*, copyright © 1963 by Libby Hillman, published by Hearthside Press. Used by permission of the author.

Contents

·

Preface

I N case you are wondering why I decided to write a Russian cookbook, the original reason was to make my last semester of high school more interesting. The inspiration came when I was wondering if there was such a thing as Russian cooking. I was extremely perturbed to discover that there most certainly was and I didn't know about it. I didn't even connect beef Stroganoff and *borscht* with Russian cooking. I thought beef Stroganoff was the invention of a frozen food company, and *borscht* was a thin red liquid bought in jars. Then to discover beef Stroganoff is not served on noodles and should not have mushrooms and tomato paste, and that *borscht* can be a hearty meal by itself!

That's how it all started. The ultimate goal of my project became to learn about the geographical, historical, cultural, and religious background of Russia through its cooking. I had difficulty finding books on the culture itself and the day-to-day life, and so a lot of my ideas are extrapolations.

They may not be perfect—but I'd like to share them with you just in case they approach the truth. I've made an attempt to catch the religious customs before they completely disappear, and my information is from "primary" sources—I spoke to a Russian Orthodox priest from Long Island, and read a British traveler's journal from the early 1900's.

I've done my best to present accurate information on customs, and authentic, unadulterated, workable, and delicious recipes—and if I've made any bloopers, first forgive me, and then send me a polite note.

In general, this book is very dedicated. But I'd like to reserve a hunk of the dedication to Joyce Vining Morgan and her family, for giving me encouragement, help, advice, a kitchen, and mouths, and for putting up with my adolescent idiosyncrasies for five months. Another slab of dedication should be reserved for Mom and Dad. And then the rest to all the other people who helped me eat it all. Anyone else who would like a piece of dedication, help yourself—there's plenty to go around. You can even have seconds.

JANE BLANKSTEEN

Introduction

THE Soviet Union consists of fifteen different republics and countless linguistic groups. The land borders on Europe, Scandinavia, Greece, Turkey, Iran, Afghanistan, Pakistan, and China. As a result of this physical arrangement, the cooking styles vary according to the climate and the geographical situation.

Russian cooking shows the influence of its climate. The fear that winter might come too early and leave too late, and thus shorten the already short growing season, influenced the development of cuisine that makes extensive use of pickling and drying.

It was common to be trapped indoors for several days at a time after a sudden winter blizzard, and so many Russian dishes readily make use of leftovers. An example of this is *piroshky*, little pies stuffed with meat or vegetables or cheese—whatever you have left over. Other examples of "leftover" dishes are the improvisational soups, which improve with age.

In Old Russia, milk and cream were not pasteurized as they are today. Unpasteurized milk sours more quickly than pasteurized milk, but the soured product was not thrown away because it was still edible. Sour cream is used extensively in Russian cooking; in fact, a popular Russian breakfast is sour cream sweetened with coarse sugar.

The history of Russian cooking can be traced back to 700 B.C. The Oriental influence in Russian cooking probably originated with the Scythians and Mongolian foot soldiers who entered Russia because they had been pushed out from Central Asia by Chinese expansion in 700 B.C. These Scythians were the ruling aristocracy in Russia for five hundred years.

The Goths, a Germanic people, arrived in the valley of the Vistula in 200 A.D. because population pressure in Scandinavia forced them to emigrate. Later, in 862 A.D., the Scandinavian prince Rurik became the first Czar of Russia. Scandinavian influence on Russian cooking is manifested in the fruit soups, and the hors d'oeuvres, *zakoosky*, which are similar to the Scandinavian smorgasbord. Another example of influence (although I don't know who started it first) is the Russian Easter bread, *kulich*; it is very similar to the Finnish Easter bread, the only difference being that the Russians use some rye flour instead of all white flour.

Missionaries from the Greek Orthodox Church converted Russians to Christianity in the tenth century. Perhaps this is when *shashlyk*, a skewered meat dish similar to *shish kebab*, became part of the Russian diet.

If the Scythians didn't manage to influence Russian cooking with Oriental techniques, the Mongol invasion under Genghis Khan in the thirteenth century must have. Perhaps that is when *pelmeny*, little dumplings similar to the Chinese wonton, became a part of Siberian cooking.

German influence on Russian cooking came with Peter the

Great's campaign to open the "windows to the west," in the early 1700's. Sausage, sauerkraut, and *schnitzel* are often found on Russian menus.

French influence came with Catherine II's reign in the eighteenth century. St. Petersburg society, as described in Tolstoy's novels, show the effects of Catherine's love for the French. She loved their language, their dress, and their food. In Tolstoy's day, rich "princes" always had their own imported French chefs. Beef Stroganoff was the invention of Count Stroganoff's chef. Salat Olivier was the invention of a Russian noble's imported French chef, who had to prepare a quick meal for some surprise guests.

Almost every Russian novel alludes to the enormous Russian appetite and the generous Russian hospitality; to accept the latter is to possess the former! At the very least guests are greeted with bread and salt—the traditional sign of hospitality and happiness. To describe the Russian appetite, I've found no one more qualified to speak than Gogol:

> The author [Gogol] . . . is quite unimpressed by the high-living set of Petersburg and Moscow who spend their time planning what they will eat tomorrow and what dinner they should order for the day after, who sit down to a meal without first dispatching some pill, who then devour oysters, sea spiders, and other marine wonders, after which they head for Carlsbad or the spas of the Caucasus to recover. No, these gentry have never aroused his envy. But he is envious of certain persons of intermediary status who at one way station will order ham, at the next suckling pig, at a third a slice of sturgeon or salami with garlic, after which, as though they hadn't eaten a thing, they'll sit down at any time and have fish soup with eels and roe and everything in it, which hisses and gurgles in

their mouths, followed by all sorts of pies, all of which is enough to make even an onlooker hungry—well, these people have an enviable, heaven-sent gift indeed!

. . . the Madeira scorched the mouth because the merchants . . . doctored it mercilessly with rum and sometimes even added state-monopoly vodka to it, trusting Russian stomachs to cope with anything that came along.

FROM *Dead Souls*

NOTHING BEETS
BORSCHT

Breakfasts

(ZAVTRAK)

BREAKFAST in Russia is not a monumental affair. It is simple but good. The reason the Russians don't make very large breakfasts is that they like to gently work their way up to the climax, which is dinner. Breakfast is called *zavtrak*, which comes from the Russian word that means "tomorrow." (I don't know what that has to do with anything.)

A Russian breakfast is more of a little snack to quiet your stomach than it is a full meal. Russians sometimes eat eggs: sometimes cooked, sometimes raw. The cooked eggs are usually in omelet form with black bread or with vegetables. The raw eggs are often eaten right out of the shell: My Russian grandmother pokes a small hole in one end of the eggshell with a needle, and then sucks out the egg. She says it's delicious.

If it's not eggs for breakfast, it's toast, jam, and tea, or perhaps a glass of sour cream with castor sugar, or some other dairy products.

Breakfast in Russian hotels, designed for foreign tourists, is elaborate. For instance, a typical breakfast menu would include a full line of *zakoosky*—ham, cheese, sardines, sprats, sturgeon, etc. Then there would be a glass of *kefir*, sour cream, or *prostokvasha*; and then eggs, or *sirniky*, or *bliny* (see pages 130–134).

RUSSIAN YOGURT
(*Prostokvasha*)

This is the Russian counterpart of yogurt. *Prostokvasha* tastes much richer, and better (in my opinion, of course). It takes a full twenty-four hours to get cultured (that's a euphemism for "soured," which is another euphemism for "a little bit rotten"), so if you want to have it for breakfast—plan ahead.

Because of the shortage of food, and in the old days the shortage of refrigerators, soured milk products became very popular in Russia. This is one of them. It is often served with castor sugar or with jam to sweeten it.

Plain or skimmed milk may be used instead of cream.

(PER PERSON)

½ *cup heavy cream*
½ *cup milk*
1 *tablespoon sour cream*

Put the heavy cream and milk in a pot, stir, and then bring to a boil. Immediately remove from heat. Let it cool to lukewarm. Then stir in the sour cream.

Cover the pot with a towel and set in a warm draft-free place (like an unlit oven) for at least 24 hours.

RUSSIAN BUTTERMILK
(*Kefir*)

Kefir is almost always served for breakfast. It is a super-thick buttermilk, which, at its best, is too thick to pour out of a bottle.

In Russia, all the milk stores sell *kefir*. Sometimes you can buy it in bottles—but then you pay as much for the bottle as you do for the *kefir*. Most Russians bring their own containers, and have their morning's supply of *kefir* ladled out of a big vat.

Plain or skimmed milk may be used instead of cream.

(PER PERSON)

½ *cup heavy cream*
½ *cup milk*
1 *tablespoon buttermilk*

Bring heavy cream and milk to the boil. Remove from heat immediately.

Let the milk and cream cool to lukewarm. Then stir in the tablespoon of buttermilk. Cover with a towel and leave in a draft-free place (like an unlit oven) for at least 24 hours.

RUSSIAN CURD CHEESE
WITH SOUR CREAM
(*Tvorog so Smetanoy*)

A popular Russian breakfast is a plate with a mound of sweetened curd cheese accompanied by a spoonful of sour cream. The conventional substitute for Russian curd cheese, called *tvorog*, is pot cheese or a dry cottage cheese. When I was in the Soviet Union, however, my immediate reaction to *tvorog* was that it tasted like a cross between farmer's cheese and cream cheese. When I returned to New York, I bought those cheeses and experimented until I came up with the "right" proportion. The following is what I decided was the right proportion. Even if it isn't just right, it is great for making *sirniky*, the cheese pancakes that are also served for breakfast (see the next recipe).

(2 TO 4 SERVINGS, DEPENDING ON STATE OF HUNGER)

¾ *pound farmer's cheese*
¼ *pound cream cheese*
   Sugar to taste
3 *to* 4 *tablespoons sour cream* (or kefir, or prostokvasha)

Put the cheeses in a bowl and mix them together, using the back of a spoon, until the mixture is smooth.
Add sugar to taste.
Serve in a mound on a plate with a dollop of sour cream on top. *Kefir* or *prostokvasha* can be used instead of sour cream.

CHEESE PANCAKES
(*Sirniky*)

The Russian word for cheese is *sir*—hence the name *sirniky* for these cheese patties. They are also called *tvorozhniky*, from the Russian word *tvorog*, meaning "curd cheese," but they are most often called *sirniky*.

Sirniky are served for breakfast with sour cream and sugar. Many food shops in Russia, called *kulinarias*, sell them ready made, so that all you have to do is brown them. They are extremely simple to make, but since most people in Russia work, there is little time for home cooking.

The cheese used for *sirniky* is *tvorog* (see preceding recipe). If you can't get farmer's cheese (or pot cheese) to make the *tvorog* part of this recipe, use cottage cheese, letting it drain a few hours in a cloth-lined sieve.

(PER PERSON)

3 *ounces farmer's cheese*
1 *ounce cream cheese*
1 *egg, beaten*
2 *tablespoons flour*
1 *teaspoon sugar (or to taste)*
Flour, butter

Put the cheeses into a small mixing bowl and with the back of a spoon cream them together so they form a smooth mixture.

Mix 1 tablespoon of the beaten egg into the cheese, then mix the flour in gradually, and finally add the sugar.

Form the cheese into a patty, like a hamburger, and coat it

with flour. By the way, this will be sort of sticky, but the flour coating will make it possible to form the cheese into a nice round shape.

Brush the patty on both sides with some of the leftover beaten egg and coat again with flour.

Heat a frying pan, melt some butter, and over a low-medium flame brown the *sirniky* patty on both sides.

Serve hot with some sour cream and sugar, or with jam.

BREAKFAST ROLLS
(*Boolichky*)

These are round rolls, made from Irina's basic *piroshky* dough and spiked with raisins. Every morning these rolls were on the table next to the black bread and butter.

Irina's piroshky *dough, risen and punched down, ready for shaping (see page 214).*
1 *cup or more raisins*

GLAZE: 1 *egg*
      1 *teaspoon cream or milk*

Divide the dough into 8 to 10 parts or more, depending upon how big you want the rolls to be. In Russia they are at least 4 inches in diameter.

Take a tablespoon of raisins (more or less, according to taste), and work them into each piece of dough while kneading. Shape the piece of dough into a ball. Flatten it slightly and place on a buttered cookie sheet. Let rise for 20 to 30 minutes and then brush with an egg beaten with a teaspoon of cream or milk. Bake at 350° F. for ½ hour, or until a deep golden brown.

Serve with butter and jam.

WHITE BREAD AND BEET JAM

A typical Russian breakfast might be a thick slice of home-baked white bread with homemade jam, like beet preserves, the recipe for which follows this one.

Uncle Peter would bring an enormous crust of white bread and a large earthenware jar of home-made jam. He would slice the bread, smear it liberally with jam, and hold out the tasty slices in the palms of his hands as he offered them to the guests with a low bow.

"Please do have some," he said invitingly, and whenever anybody took a slice he would look closely at his palm, and lick any drops of jam that were left there.

FROM GORKY, *My Childhood*

WHITE BREAD
(*Byellee Hlyeb*)

This dough can be used to make rolls or large loaves.
(Rolls are called *boolichky*.)

(4 MEDIUM-SIZED LOAVES)

2 packages dry yeast or 1
 ounce fresh yeast
1 teaspoon sugar
2½ cups lukewarm water
6 cups white flour
2 tablespoons honey
4 tablespoons butter

2 teaspoons salt
Approximately 1 cup flour,
 to flour the board
Vegetable oil
Cornmeal
Sesame, poppy, or caraway
 seeds (optional)

GLAZE: *water and cornstarch or egg white*

Dissolve the yeast and sugar in the ½ cup lukewarm water in a big bowl.

Gradually beat in 2 cups of white flour, 1½ cups of lukewarm water, and the honey and butter. Beat vigorously or use your hands if you don't have a machine.

Add another 4 cups of white flour gradually while you are still beating.

Add another ½ cup of lukewarm water and the salt. Keep beating until the dough leaves the sides of the bowl.

Remove the dough from the bowl (it is rather sticky) and knead it thoroughly on a floured board until it is smooth and elastic. This should take about 10 minutes.

Shape the dough into a round ball and place in a greased bowl (use a little bit of vegetable oil). Turn the ball of dough over once or twice to get both sides of the dough greasy.

Cover the bowl with plastic wrap and then with a terrycloth towel. Let the dough rise in a warm place until it has doubled in bulk. This takes about an hour. (A good place to put it is an unlit oven.)

When the dough has risen, punch it down and turn it out onto a lightly floured board. Cut it into 2, 3, or 4 parts, depending on the size loaves you want to make. If you make rolls, then divide it even smaller.

Knead each piece of dough lightly, just enough to make it firm enough to mold into a nice, smooth-surfaced shape. You can make them round, oval—anything that appeals to you: the dough needs no pan.

Sprinkle a cookie sheet with cornmeal and place the loaves or rolls on it—keep them at a distance from each other because they will double in bulk once more. I have personally produced Siamese twins and they are not very attractive—so don't be stingy for space.

Before you set the loaves to rise, take a single-edged razor blade, or a sharp knife, and slash the bread. Long loaves look nice with horizontal slashes. Round loaves look nice with a giant asterisk (*) shape or an X. Now let the dough rise for about 30 to 40 minutes. Meanwhile preheat the oven to 400° F.

When the bread has risen, place a pan of hot tap water on the lowest rack of the oven. Brush the bread with warm water. Bake for 15 minutes at 400° F.

Lower the oven heat to 350° F. and bake for another 25 minutes.

Brush the loaves with an egg white mixed with 1 teaspoon cold water, or with 1 tablespoon cornstarch mixed with ½ cup warm water. They both will yield a crunchy crust—I prefer the egg white, some people prefer the cornstarch, and since it's a very touchy matter, I leave the final decision up to you.

Before you put the bread back in the oven to bake again, re-move the pan of water. Then let the bread bake for another 10 minutes, until the glaze is dry (at this point you can sprin-kle sesame or poppy or caraway seeds on top of the loaves).

Cool the loaves on a rack.

BEET PRESERVES

(FROM LOUISE MCGRATH, WHO GOT IT FROM KATHERINE ALEXEIEFF)

This is like a marmalade except it is made with beets. I would like to give this recipe a star, or something, because it is not just another jam—it is . . .

Sorry, I've been trying to think of an uncorny word to de-scribe something that tastes good, but I haven't come up with anything. Let it suffice to say: *Try it.*

(2 CUPS)

> 2 *pounds beets (large, tough beets can be used)*
> *Boiling water*
> 4 *cups sugar*
> 1 *tablespoon ground ginger*
> 1 *cup slivered or coarsely chopped almonds*
> 2 *juicy lemons (medium-sized)*

Put the washed, but unpeeled, beets in a pot, cover them with boiling water, and simmer until they are tender. This will take about an hour—more or less depending on the size of the beets.

Rinse the cooked beets with cold water until they are cool,

so that you can handle them without causing any serious damage to the skin on your hands. You should then be able to slip the beet skin off the beet without much trouble.

When you have skinned the beets, dice them into ¼-inch cubes.

Put the beets into a *waterless* pot with the sugar, ginger, and almonds. Stir this mixture so that the beets are evenly coated with the sugar and ginger and the almonds are well distributed.

Put the pot over a very tiny flame and cook uncovered for ½ hour, stirring every now and then to keep it from burning.

After the ½ hour is up, chop the lemons very fine, peel and all; discard any seeds. Add the lemon to the pot. Continue cooking for another ½ hour.

Give this mixture a jelly test at this point: Put a tiny bit of jelly onto a plate and let it stand for 5 minutes. If it jells—test by running your finger through it; if it wrinkles up it is jelled—then pour the jam into hot, dry jars. Let stand until they cool, then cover and seal the jars. If you know nothing about sealing jars, use old jars from commercial jellies and jams, or just keep it refrigerated.

Russians serve this in little glass saucers with their tea, or it can be used to spread on delicious white bread, such as the one in the preceding recipe.

Lunches

(VTOROYEH ZAVTRAK)

I N Russia, lunch is a three-course dinner, and dinner is a two-course lunch. For practical purposes I have reversed the order in this book.

The samovar tradition, sitting around all evening eating cakes and tea, made robust dinners obsolete. That is why lunch became the larger of the two meals.

> # MENU
>
> *Yerevan-style Chicken*
> *or Chicken Chakhokbily*
> *Pot Cheese Pudding*

YEREVAN-STYLE CHICKEN
(*Kooritsa po yerevansky*)

A word about Yerevan . . .

Yerevan is the capital of the Armenian Republic of the U.S.S.R. It is a cultural center and one of the oldest cities of the Caucasus. This is a hot and dry area; irrigation, however, has made the cultivation of vineyards and orchards possible; in fact, wine and canned fruit are some of the city's main products. It seems logical, then, that Yerevan-style chicken includes fruits.

It is very simple to make; the dish is browned chicken parts simmered in onions, raisins, prunes, and stock.

An interesting Caucasian technique is to brown the chicken in sour cream (see pressed chicken [*tabaka*] and pork chops with cherry or prune sauce [pages 82 and 103]). This method both locks the juices of the meat and gives it a beautiful golden color.

NOTES:

1. The original recipe did not call for wine—but it is a nice addition. You can substitute white wine for the stock in whole or in part.

2. Use fryers, or spring chickens—that is, little chickens—or the meat won't cook all the way through and will be tough.

3. This recipe will serve four—about ¾ pound of chicken per person. If you plan to serve more than 4 pounds of chicken, you may need two frying pans with covers.

4. In case you forgot to or couldn't buy pitted prunes: Pour boiling water over the prunes and let them soak for 2 to 3 minutes. Then, with a small knife, make a slit in each prune and remove the pit.

(4 SERVINGS)

2 onions, chopped fine
2 tablespoons butter
2 2-pound chickens, cut up
1 cup (8 ounces) sour cream
  Salt and pepper

1 cup or 8 ounces pitted prunes
1 cup or 6 ounces golden raisins
1 cup chicken stock and/or
  white wine

Sauté the chopped onions in 1 tablespoon butter in a large frying pan that has a cover. (Cover is not needed yet.) When they are lightly browned, remove from pan and put aside in a small dish or bowl.

Brush the skin side of each piece of chicken with enough sour cream to coat it lightly.

Add another tablespoon of butter to the onion pan and when it has melted, put all the chicken parts skin side down in the pan.

Salt and pepper the naked side of the chicken parts and then brush them with sour cream, using just enough sour cream to coat the surface lightly.

When the skin side is golden brown, turn chicken parts over and then when the second side is brown . . .

Put the sautéed onions over the chicken, then the prunes and raisins, and finally the chicken stock and/or wine.

Cover the pan and let simmer for ½ hour or until the chicken is cooked.

Serve.

CHICKEN CHAKHOKBILY   *Kooritsa Chakhokbily*

Chicken *chakhokbíly*, a Georgian version of chicken *cacciatore*, is supposed to have been Josef Stalin's favorite dish. This little note is meant to stimulate your intellectual curiosity—not your emotions.

This variation on chicken *Yerevan* is cooked exactly the same way except that there are no prunes, raisins, and white wine; in other words, the sauce is completely different.

(4 TO 6 SERVINGS)

2 *onions, chopped fine*
2 *tablespoons butter*
2 *2-pound chickens, cut up*
1 *cup (8 ounces) sour cream*
4 *small tomatoes, peeled and chopped*
2 *tablespoons lemon juice*

2 *to 3 tablespoons minced fresh dill*
½ *cup chicken stock*
½ *cup Madeira or dry Port wine*
3 *tablespoons tomato puree*

Proceed with the browning of onion and chicken as described in the preceding recipe.

When the chicken pieces have been browned, pour in the onions, tomatoes, lemon juice, dill, stock, wine, and tomato purée. Simmer, covered, for ½ hour or until chicken is done.

POT CHEESE PUDDING
(*Zapyekanka eez Tvoroga*)

Zapyekanka means a baked pudding and *eez tvoroga* means "of curd cheese"; so this dessert is a baked pot (or cottage) cheese pudding. The cheese is sweetened, sieved, and combined with dried fruits and lightened with eggs. It tastes like the filling of an excellent light cheese cake. It can be served hot or cold. I prefer it cold—no particular reason; I just do.

NOTES:

1. Pot cheese, a drier version of cottage cheese, should be used for this recipe. If it is not available, farmer's cheese may be substituted, or the cottage cheese may be wrapped in cheesecloth or gauze and placed in a sieve, over a bowl, with a heavy weight on top of the cheese. If left to drip for 3 hours, the cottage cheese should be dry enough.

2. *Zapyekanka* keeps well in the refrigerator, so make it in advance if you need to. It should last about a week.

(4 TO 6 SERVINGS)

3 tablespoons unsalted butter
1 pound pot cheese
4 egg yolks, beaten
½ cup sugar
¼ cup minus 2 teaspoons semolina or farina

¼ cup raisins and/or golden raisins (citron and candied peel are often added)
Rind of one lemon, grated
4 egg whites
¼ teaspoon lemon juice
Pinch of salt

Bring 8 cups of water, salted, to a boil. Add the bones and meat and bring to a boil again. Cover and simmer for ½ hour.

Meanwhile, sauté the chopped onions and garlic in butter in a large frying pan until they are soft, but not brown. Add the carrots and brown them. Add the celery and brown it also. Finally, add the sauerkraut, brown sugar, and lemon juice. Cover the pan and let simmer for ½ hour.

During the time the vegetables are simmering, the broth will be ready. Skim off the scum. Remove the marrow from the marrow bones and put it back in the broth. Discard the bones. Let the broth sit on a very low flame, covered, until the vegetables are ready.

Add the vegetables to the broth and sprinkle in some pepper. Bring the soup to a boil, then let it simmer gently, partially covered, for 1½ hours. Bring it to a rolling boil again, then partially cover and let it simmer for another hour.

Transfer the soup to small ceramic pots, individual soufflé dishes, or one large soufflé dish.

To serve:

Preheat oven to 350° F.

Roll out half a batch of sour-cream dough on a well-floured board to a ¼-inch thickness. Cover each pot with a piece of dough that is draped over the edge.

Bake the pots or pot 20 to 30 minutes or until the pastry is a nice golden brown.

Serve with a sauceboat of sour cream sprinkled with chopped fresh dill.

Enjoy.

BUCKWHEAT CAKES
(*Kroopyenik*)

(RECIPE FROM THE INTOURIST RESTAURANT, MOSCOW)

(4 SERVINGS—2 SQUARES EACH)

1 *cup uncooked buckwheat groats*
6 *ounces farmer's cheese or pot cheese*
2 *ounces cream cheese*

¼ *cup sugar*
3 *eggs, separated*
Pinch of salt
Butter

Cook the buckwheat groats as for *kasha* (see page 195) using water instead of stock.

Cream the two cheeses together in a bowl with the back of a spoon.

Mix the cheese, sugar, and cooked groats thoroughly.

Beat the egg yolks slightly and combine with the cheese–sugar–groat mixture.

Beat the egg whites with a pinch of salt until soft peaks hold when the beater or whisk is lifted from the bowl.

Fold the whites into the cheese mixture.

Butter a rectangular pan that's about 5 by 7 inches.

Pour the mixture into the pan and spread it out so that it is about ½ inch thick.

Bake at 400° F. for ½ hour, or until the top is brown, and, when a knife is inserted into it, it comes out clean and dry.

Cut into squares and serve.

APPLE PIE MADE OF AIR
(*Vozdooshny Pirog*)

This dessert is a cross between an apple meringue and an apple soufflé. It is served hot, fresh from the oven, before it falls. It is important to put this in a soufflé dish that holds just the amount you make; otherwise it will sink.

To make it for company, have the purée made in advance, and the eggs separated. Then put it in the oven while the main course is being eaten. Don't forget that the oven must be preheated. In case you do forget, and have the pie ready for the oven, cover it tightly with plastic wrap and it won't sink while the oven is preheating.

Russians don't traditionally serve the *vozdooshny pirog* this way, but it tastes nice with a cold sauce made with the leftover yolks—Gogol-Mogol sauce. The sauce is Russian—and very much like the French *crème anglaise*. When my mother was a little kid, and got sick, my grandmother would give her what she remembers as "guggle-muggle." Apparently my grandmother was not such a great "guggle-muggle" maker, because both my mother and her brother remember it as a threat—sort of like cod-liver oil.

Apple purée:

(1½ CUPS)

    6 apples
    2 tablespoons unsalted butter
    Juice of half a small lemon—2 tablespoons
    2 tablespoons Calvados (apple brandy) or Grand
        Marnier

¼ to ½ cup of sugar (to taste, or depending on sweetness of
the apples)
1 cinnamon stick

Peel and core the apples. Then slice them very thin.

Melt the butter in a frying pan that has a cover, and when it is foaming put the apple slices in the pan. Make sure the flame is very low.

When the apples have softened, and the edges have browned slightly, add the lemon juice and Calvados or Grand Marnier, sprinkle on the sugar, and lay the cinnamon stick on top.

When the sugar begins to glaze the apples, cover the pan and let it steam for about 10 minutes. By that time the apples should be a flavorful mush.

Remove the apples from the pan and put them in a bowl. Mash the apples with a wooden spoon to make a smooth purée.

The soufflé:

(4 SERVINGS)

6 egg whites
Pinch of salt, drop of lemon juice
1½ cups apple purée

Preheat the oven to 400° F.

Beat the egg whites with the salt and lemon juice, using a wire whisk, until they hold firm peaks when the beater is lifted out of the bowl.

Fold the whites into the purée, and then pour the mixture into a 1-quart buttered-and-sugared soufflé dish. (To butter and sugar the dish: First butter the dish, then put some sugar in and shake it around, so the sides and bottom are coated.)

Bake for 20 to 30 minutes, until a wire tester, when stuck in the middle of the soufflé, comes out clean. The top should be lightly browned.

Serve immediately with a pitcher of Gogol-Mogol sauce.

GOGOL-MOGOL SAUCE

Ukrainians serve this sauce with walnuts, as a dessert in itself.

6 *egg yolks*
2 *tablespoons sugar*
2 *teaspoons Calvados (apple brandy), or rum, or vanilla extract*

In a small pot, set in a pan of water over a low flame (that is, a double boiler), whisk the yolks, sugar, and brandy, rum or vanilla extract. Whisk until the yolks turn a pale yellow and/or the mixture is *lukewarm*, not hot.

Remove from heat, put into a serving bowl, and chill until needed.

MENU

Borscht

Cheese Tarts
or Ukrainian Garlic Rolls
Apple Charlotte

BEET SOUP
Borscht

Borscht originated in the Ukraine; its name is the old Slavonic word for "beet." There are unlimited variations, and, like *shchee*, it is a "hatchet soup." The ingredients vary from region to region—sometimes the *borscht* will have a lot of meat and will be more like a stew—a good hot lunch for a cold winter day—and sometimes it's mostly vegetables.

Borscht is served with a sour cream dollop in each bowl (never add the sour cream to the pot), and *vatrooshky*—little open-faced cheese tarts.

TYPES OF BORSCHT   The Ukraine has a huge beet crop, and so their *borscht* has a high proportion of beets—especially in the western Ukraine, where beets sometimes are the only vegetable in the *borscht*.

Central Ukrainians tend to add a lot of cabbage to theirs.

Poltavians use goose bones and flesh for the stock; other parts of the Ukraine use pork, ham, and bacon.

The famous "Moscow *borscht*" is not exclusively beets; it is more of a vegetable soup. A typical preparation would include carrots, potatoes, beets, tomatoes, parsnips, cabbage, onions, garlic. It does, however, have a deep red color.

Northern Russians use beef stock for the soup base.

Byelorussians use at least three kinds of meat for their stock.

Odessa-style *borscht* has green pepper in it and a larger proportion of tomatoes than most *borscht*.

The specific *borscht* recipes included here are contrasting styles. The first is a very hearty Ukrainian *borscht*, with sausage and ham. It is served with garlic rolls called *pampooshky*. The second is made with prunes and beef and has a sweet and sour taste. *Vatrooshky*—open-faced *piroshky* with a cheese filling— often accompany it. When I made it, it was fed to a group of sixteen- and seventeen-year-old boys (my adviser's advisees, who liked both but declared the Ukrainian *borscht* the winner. I liked both, but I have a weakness for prunes.

NOTES ON ALL BORSCHT:

1. *Borscht* freezes and refrigerates well.

2. *Borscht* improves with age. It probably should not be served the day it is made.

3. Russians add sour salt to the *borscht* to make it a little bit tangy. This can be obtained in old-fashioned Jewish delicatessens. However, if you can't find it, a few tablespoons of vinegar or lemon juice will do.

4. The red glow may fade—and most likely will; so keep an extra raw beet around and peel it, then grate it into a little cold water or cold red wine, about half a cup. This liquid will be bright red and should be added to the soup before serving.

5. Peel the beets and remove the greens before grating them.

6. A note on buying beets—larger ones are easier to handle but not as sweet as smaller ones. I suggest using larger beets and adding some sugar to the pot (1 tablespoon). You can judge a beet by its greens: they shouldn't be limp. The beets should be firm. Canned beets may be used. In fact they have a nicer color. But fresh beets taste better.

UKRAINIAN BORSCHT

Stock:

(10 TO 12 SERVINGS)

3 *pounds ham hock*	1 *carrot, peeled*
1 *bay leaf*	1 *celery stalk*
1 *onion, peeled and studded*	*Salt and pepper*
with 5 cloves	3 *quarts water*

Stock Method:

1. Put all the ingredients in a large soup pot and bring liquid to a boil.

2. Turn off the heat and skim off the scum on the surface of the soup. The scum is that foamy, muddy stuff reminiscent of the foam you are likely to find at a polluted beach.

3. Now, cover the pot—partially—and let the soup simmer for 3 hours.

4. After 3 hours are up, let the soup cool. When it is cool enough not to scald your fingers, remove the vegetables and bay leaf and the ham hock.

5. Throw out the vegetables and bay leaf, but save the ham

hock. Remove all the meat from the bones and shred it with your fingers; throw out the bones.

6. Put the shredded meat in the pot.

7. Refrigerate the stock and, before you are about to use it, skim the fat off the top. It will be a solid white layer covering the stock.

NOTE:

Stock can be kept frozen for ages. It can also be kept on the back burner of your stove for a few days, if you bring it to a boil once in the morning and once in the evening to prevent any bacteria from being fruitful and multiplying.

Borscht:

1 *medium onion, minced*
1 *clove garlic, minced*
2 *slices bacon or some butter or shortening*
2 *small carrots or 1 large, peeled and sliced into small disks*
1 *peeled, diced turnip or parsnip*
1 *cup peeled, chopped tomatoes or 4 small ones (can be canned)*
Salt, pepper, 1 tablespoon red wine vinegar

1 *pound beets, making 2½ cups when peeled and grated*
1 *pound white cabbage, shredded*
1 *pound potatoes, peeled and diced*
1 *pound* kolbasa *sausage or any cooked sausage you like (If you use raw sausage, first broil it or it will fall apart in the soup.)*

Optional

Russians usually add a grated parsley root and a celery root along with the grated beets. If you can find either or both— throw them in.

Borscht Method:

1. Prepare all the ingredients as directed.

2. Sauté the onion and garlic (until they are limp and white, not browned) with 2 slices of bacon or just butter.

3. Sauté, adding to the onions and bacon or butter, the carrots, turnip, tomatoes (parsley and celery roots), salt, pepper, and vinegar.

4. Add 2 cups of stock to the frying pan with the vegetables.

5. Then add the beets. Cover the pan and simmer for 45 minutes.

6. Meanwhile, bring the 2 quarts of stock to a boil, then add the shredded cabbage and diced potatoes and simmer for 15 minutes.

7. When the beets are ready, dump the entire contents of the pan into the stock.

8. Simmer, partially covered, for 15 minutes to combine flavors.

9. Season to taste—salt, pepper, sugar, vinegar.

10. Fifteen minutes before serving, add the sausage cut into the small, round slices, and simmer for 15 minutes partially covered.

GARNISH: A dollop of sour cream in each bowl and some chopped dill sprinkled on top. Serve with *pampooshky*.

UKRAINIAN GARLIC ROLLS
(*Pampooshky*)

I got this recipe from the chef at the Hotel Ukraine in Kiev. I'm still not clear whether he said it was for *shchee*, or *sol-*

yanka, or *borscht.* Things can get sort of confusing when talking to an excited and efferverscent chef who doesn't speak a word of English. At any rate, I have decided that this should be served with Ukrainian *borscht,* partly because I saw it in a picture in a Kiev guidebook, but mostly because I had nothing else to serve with Ukrainian *borscht.*

Buy those great, soft, eggy dinner rolls that come in the form of multiple Siamese twins, and heat and serve them with the following dressing poured over.

The dressing:

> ¼ *cup sunflower oil*
> 1 *clove garlic, smashed and chopped fine*
> *Salt to taste*
> *Chopped fresh parsley to taste*

BORSCHT WITH PRUNES

Stock:

(10 TO 12 SERVINGS)

2 *to* 3 *pounds marrow bones*	1 *carrot*
3 *pounds beef flanken*	1 *bay leaf*
1 *onion studded with cloves*	*Salt and pepper*
1 *parsnip*	1 *ounce dried mushrooms*
1 *stalk celery*	3 *quarts water*

Stock Method:

1. Put all the ingredients in a large soup pot and bring liquid to a boil.

2. Turn off the heat and skim off the scum on the surface of the soup. The scum is that foamy, muddy stuff reminiscent of the foam you are likely to find at a polluted beach.

3. Now, cover the pot—partially—and let the soup simmer for 3 hours.

4. After 3 hours are up, let the soup cool. When it is cool enough not to scald your fingers, remove the vegetables and bay leaf and the soup beef.

5. Throw out the vegetables and bay leaf, but save the soup beef. Remove all the meat from the bones and shred it with your fingers; throw out the bones.

6. Put the shredded meat in the pot.

7. Refrigerate the stock and, before you are about to use it, skim the fat off the top. It will be a solid white layer covering the stock.

NOTE:

Stock can be kept frozen for ages. It can also be kept on the back burner of your stove for a few days, if you bring it to a boil once in the morning and once in the evening to prevent any bacteria from being fruitful and multiplying.

Borscht:

1 onion, chopped fine
1 clove garlic, chopped fine
Butter
2 carrots, sliced
2 tomatoes, coarsely chopped
Salt and pepper
1 teaspoon red wine vinegar

1 pound beets, making 2½ cups when peeled and grated
¾ pound white cabbage, shredded
1 teaspoon sugar
½ pound pitted prunes, chopped

Borscht Method:

1. Prepare all the ingredients as directed.

2. Sauté the onions and garlic (until they are limp and white, not browned) with butter.

3. Sauté, adding to the onions and butter, the carrots, tomatoes, salt, pepper, and vinegar.

4. Add 2 cups of stock to the frying pan with the vegetables.

5. Then add the beets. Cover the pan and simmer for 45 minutes.

6. Meanwhile, bring the 2 quarts of stock to a boil, then add the shredded cabbage and simmer for 15 minutes.

7. When the beets are ready, dump the entire contents of the pan into the stock.

8. Simmer, partially covered, for 15 minutes to combine flavors.

9. Season to taste—salt, pepper, sugar, vinegar.

GARNISH: *a dollop of sour cream in each bowl and some chopped dill sprinkled on top. Serve with* vatrooshky.

CHEESE TARTS
(*Vatrooshky*)

(16 *vatrooshky*–8 SERVINGS)

Filling:

1½ *pounds farmer's cheese (or pot cheese)*
½ *pound cream cheese*
2 *egg yolks*
1 *egg white*
 Sugar to taste (4 to 8 tablespoons)

Cream the cheeses together in a bowl with a wooden spoon. If using pot cheese, you may find it necessary to sieve the cheese. The object is to make this a smooth mixture.

Thoroughly mix in the egg yolks, egg white and sugar.

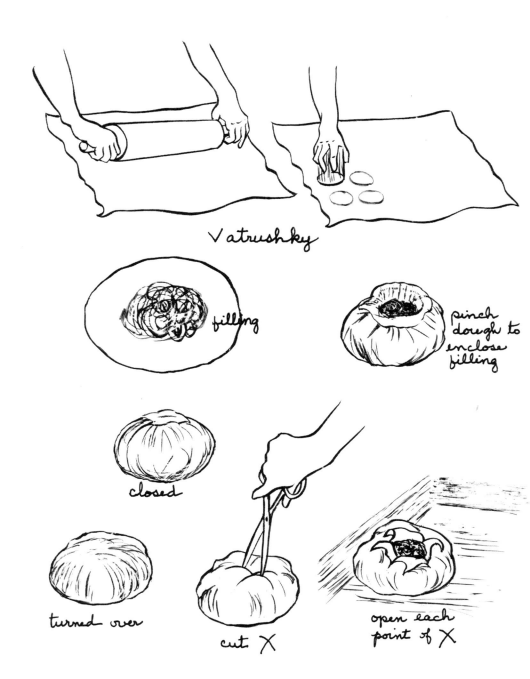

Vatrushky

filling

pinch
dough to
enclose
filling

closed

turned over

cut X

open each
point of X

Assembly:

> 1 *batch* Irina's piroshky *dough (page 214)*
> 1 *egg mixed with 1 teaspoon milk or cream*

Follow *piroshky* instructions exactly, except shape the *vatrooshky* into spherical rolls, and before allowing them to rise, set them on their cookie sheets and, with a scissors, snip an ✕ across the top.

Fold back the flaps exposing the top of the cheese filling. You now have an open-faced tart. Let rise for half an hour.

Brush the *vatrooshky* with the beaten egg and milk, coating both the cheese and the dough.

Bake at 350° F. until they are golden brown.

Cool on a rack covered with a damp cloth.

These can be served with *borscht*, as a tea sandwich, as a dessert, or as part of a *zakoosky* table.

APPLE CHARLOTTE
(*Yablochnaya Sharlotka*)

Yablochnaya sharlotka is a mold of alternating layers of minced apples and a black bread mixture. White bread can be used, but the true Russian apple *sharlotka* is made with black bread.

In Russia, because of the frequency of famines and the short harvest season, this dish was probably made of leftover stale bread and apples they wanted to use quickly, because they would rot soon or perhaps because there were too few apples to distribute evenly among the family. Now, *yablochnaya sharlotka* is not so much of a ruble stretcher as it is a delicious dessert.

(6 TO 8 SERVINGS)

6 crisp eating apples
   (3 pounds)
1 teaspoon lemon juice
½ cup unsalted butter
   A 1-pound loaf dark rye
   bread, slightly stale and
   with crusts removed
½ cup red wine

½ cup sugar
2 teaspoons grated orange rind
½ teaspoon vanilla extract
1 cup zwieback crumbs or
   bread crumbs
Ground cinnamon
Ground nutmeg

Peel and core the apples, cut them into thin slices, sprinkle them with lemon juice, and sauté them in a little of the butter, about 1 tablespoon.

Crumble the bread into tiny pieces and fry them lightly in the remaining butter.

Remove the bread from heat and add the wine, sugar, and orange rind. Mix well. Add the vanilla.

Grease a 9-inch-diameter high-walled pan—a *charlotte* mold if you have one, or use a spring-form pan.

Then put the zwieback or bread crumbs into the mold or pan and with a circular movement of your hand coat the bottom and sides with them. Discard excess crumbs.

Place a layer of bread mixture on the bottom of the pan and follow with a layer of apples. Sprinkle cinnamon and nutmeg over the apple layer.

If you are using a large shallow cake pan, make only one layer of apple. And now put the bread mixture on top. But if you are using a deep dish, try to make more layers; the top one should be bread. Sprinkle each apple layer with nutmeg and cinnamon.

Bake in a 300° F. oven for 1 hour.

Serve cooled or hot with the following sauce.

APRICOT SAUCE
(*Abrikovsky Sos*)

(APPROXIMATELY 2 CUPS)

1½ cups apricot preserves (12 ounces), forced through a sieve with
    the back of a spoon
2 tablespoon cold water
¼ cup brandy or rum

Add the water to the sieved apricot preserves, put in a sauce-pan, and boil for 10 minutes.

Add brandy and cook for 2 more minutes, stirring constantly.

Serve hot in a gravy boat—to be spooned onto each serving of *sharlotka*.

MENU

Circassian Chicken
Orange Rice

CIRCASSIAN CHICKEN
(*Kooritsa po Chergisky*)

Circassian chicken is made from a roasted or, more commonly, poached chicken, cut into serving pieces, served hot or cold with a nut sauce. When served cold, the nut sauce is jellied over the chicken and is delightful served on a hot summer day. In the Araquee restaurant in Leningrad, it is served cold as a *zakooska*. Personally, I prefer Circassian chicken cold—the sauce tastes better that way. It is also more convenient: it can be made in advance and taken out of the refrigerator, when you are ready to cut, with no fuss.

The Circassians belong to the Caucasian linguistic group like the Georgians. They are indigenous mountain people of the western part of the Caucasus. They are more often referred to as the Cherkess, and sometimes as the Adyge. Serving poultry with a nut sauce tends to be a trait of Caucasian cooking.

For some reason the sauce tastes better a day old, rather than fresh. Make it in advance of the rest of the dish, or make the whole dish a day or two early.

(6 SERVINGS)

1 chicken, up to 5 or 6 pounds
Butter (for roasting chicken
    and for sautéing the
    onion)
1 cup raw rice (optional)
1 small onion
3 ounces hazelnuts, blanched
    (to blanch, heat in oven;
    the skins will dry up and
    you can rub them off)
3 ounces blanched almonds

3 ounces walnuts
2 cups chicken broth
1 pinch cayenne pepper
Salt and black pepper to taste
Unflavored gelatin (only if
    using canned or instant
    chicken broth, or if your
    homemade broth is not
    strong enough; 1 envelope
    of gelatin will jell 2 cups
    of liquid)

GARNISH: fresh dill, parsley, or coriander

Roast or poach the chicken; if you poach the chicken, save the broth. Boil the rice.

Chop and sauté the onion.

Put the sautéed onion, the nuts, and 2 cups of broth in a blender. Blend at high speed until all ingredients are combined into a purée.

Season this sauce with cayenne pepper, salt, and black pepper to taste.

Dissolve a packet of gelatin in a little bit of hot water and add to the sauce.

Cut the chicken in serving pieces.

Put rice on the bottom of a serving dish (at least 2 inches deep). Arrange the chicken parts neatly on top. Pour the sauce evenly over the chicken.

Refrigerate. Serve cold, when the sauce has jelled. Garnish with your choice of fresh herbs.

ORANGE RICE
(*Rees Sapelsinamy*)

Orange rice is a great summer dessert pudding. It is served very cold, and is very refreshing. This is another one of those dishes that improves with age.

My mom retested this recipe for me, and gave some to our neighbors because she and my father couldn't eat it all. She forgot to tell them it was for dessert and I think they ate it as a salad—I'm not sure; I was too embarrassed to ask. But they liked it anyway. In other words—this can also be used as a salad —it is not exclusively a dessert.

NOTE:

Do not rinse the cooked rice with water; besides the fact that you'll rinse away vitamins (bad) and rinse away starch and gummy stuff (good), the rice will get too slippery and won't absorb the syrup.

(6 TO 8 SERVINGS)

    1 *cup raw rice*
    3 *large oranges*
    1 *orange peel*
    ½ *cup sugar*
    1⅓ *cups water*
       Pinch of ground cloves or 2 whole cloves

Boil the rice according to directions on the box, omitting the butter they suggest.

While the rice is cooling, peel the oranges, saving the peel of 1 orange.

Slice the orange into thin cross-sectional slices; the larger middle slices should then be cut in half. Arrange the slices neatly along the bottom of a nice serving bowl.

Put the rice in a mound over the oranges.

Boil, in a small saucepan, half the sugar with half the water, until it is syrupy—a few minutes.

Let the syrup cool for a little while (put it in the refrigerator if you can't stand waiting). When it has cooled down somewhat, pour the syrup over the rice.

Mince the orange peel; then put the remaining sugar and water in a saucepan with the cloves (if using whole cloves remember to remove them before using the syrup) and the orange peel. Bring this to a boil, and let it bubble for about 3 to 5 minutes. Let it cool somewhat, then pour it over the rice.

Cover the dish, or bowl, with foil or cellophane—and refrigerate.

This dessert really should be made several hours in advance or else the oranges will taste sour. I don't really mind it that way, but most people do. Serve cold, spooning out some of the rice into individual bowls and topping with some of the oranges and then some syrup.

```
┌─────────────────────────────────────┐
│                                     │
│             MENU                    │
│                                     │
│        Moscow Fish Stew             │
│     or Georgian Beef Stew           │
│        Cream of Apples              │
│                                     │
└─────────────────────────────────────┘
```

SOLYANKA

Solyanka literally means something made with salted foods. If you order *solyanka* in the Soviet Union, you will probably get a fish stew flavored with capers, Greek olives, and half-sour pickled cucumbers. Sometimes, however, you will get a meat stew, similarly prepared.

When I was in Leningrad I took a cab to my great aunt's home. The people who answered the door, however, were not my relatives, nor were they acquainted with them. They were very nice to me anyway and invited me into their apartment. It was a real hovel: a tiny apartment that housed a grandmother and mother, father, and baby boy, and others who were not present at that moment. But, no matter how poor, the Russians are always hospitable. That was one aspect of Russian culture I had read about but had never had the opportunity to see. They were lovely and warm people. We chatted, they offered me tea, they asked a lot of questions. . . . As a parting gift, they gave me a little set of recipe cards. On one side of each card is a picture of the dish, on the other side is the recipe. That's where I got the *solyanka* recipe. And it's very good.

Solyanka is a quick and inexpensive luncheon dish, and for some reason it feels appropriate for a cold winter day. I have here two types of *solyanka*—a Moscow fish *solyanka* and a Georgian meat *solyanka*.

All the ingredients can be assembled ahead of time and put in the casserole and refrigerated or frozen, so that you can just put the dish on the stove and warm it up for a quick lunch.

MOSCOW FISH STEW
(*Moscovsky Solyanka*)

(4 SERVINGS)

1 *large onion, chopped and sautéed*
1 *pound cabbage, shredded*
2 *pounds filleted halibut steak*
½ *lemon*
2 *half-sour pickled cucumbers*
   Salt and pepper
1 *cup fish stock, clam juice, or water*

4 *ounces pitted black olives*
1 *ounce capers (2 tablespoons)*
6 *tablespoons tomato purée*
2 to 4 *tablespoons bread crumbs*
4 *tablespoons grated cheese (Gouda)*
2 *tablespoons butter*

GARNISH: *black olives, sliced lemon, parsley*

If you haven't already done it, sauté the chopped onion in a large frying pan that has a cover, until lightly browned.

Add the shredded cabbage to the onions, mix, and cover the pan. Let steam over a very low flame for 15 minutes.

Cut the halibut into ¼-pound pieces or enough for individual servings and arrange them neatly over the onions and cabbage. Sprinkle with the juice of half a lemon.

Slice the two pickles (if you can't get half-sour pickles, use plain cucumbers), and arrange the slices over the fish. Salt and pepper to taste.

Pour 1 cup of stock over the fish and pickles. Cover the pot and simmer for 10 minutes. Then put 4 ounces black olives over the top of the pickles, sprinkle the capers over, and cover it all with the 6 tablespoons of tomato purée.

Cover the pot. Shake it a few times so that the tomato sauce will begin to penetrate the layers of vegetables and get to the fish. Simmer, covered, for 10 minutes. At this point you can put the dish aside until 15 minutes before you are ready to eat.

Sprinkle the top with bread crumbs, then cheese; dot with about 2 tablespoons butter. Bake, uncovered, in a 350° F. oven for about 15 minutes, or until the top is browned, the cheese melted, and the dish is warmed through.

Just before serving, decorate with lemon slices, pitted black olives, and parsley. Bring to the table in the pan.

GEORGIAN BEEF STEW
(*Groozinsky Solyanka*)

(6 SERVINGS)

Butter for sautéing and
   browning
1 cup chopped onions (2 to 3
   small ones)
1 large clove garlic, minced
3 pounds beef (chuck), cut
   into 1-inch cubes,
   trimmed of fat and
   gristle
Salt and pepper

⅓ cup dry sherry
1 cup of 1-inch new half-sour
   pickles (often sold in
   jars), sliced
4 tablespoons tomato purée
1 or more tablespoons
   chopped fresh dill
4 tablespoons sour cream
1½ cups boiled rice (for serving
   stew with)

Melt the butter in a large frying pan. When it is foaming put the chopped onions and garlic in the pan and brown them.

When the onions are browned, add the cubed beef; season with salt and pepper. Brown the meat on all sides.

Transfer browned meat and onions to a 3-quart saucepan. Do not clean the frying pan! First pour the sherry into it, heat it for a few minutes until the sherry is bubbling, and then pour it over the meat, being sure to scrape in all the brown bits from the bottom of the pan.

Add the sliced pickles, tomato puree, and chopped dill to the meat. Mix the ingredients gently. Cover the saucepan and simmer over a small flame for about 1 hour and 15 minutes. Remove from flame.

Stir in the sour cream. Then put aside until ready to eat.

To serve, heat up the *solyanka* without letting it boil and serve on a bed of boiled rice.

CREAM OF APPLES
(*Sambooka eez Yablok*)

This is a lovely, light dessert—quick and easy to make, and it refrigerates well.

A word about the apple purée used. Apple butter may be substituted, although it's very spicy. Apple sauce can also be substituted, but it tends to be too bland. The best thing is the homemade purée (see *vozdooshny pirog* [page 27] for the recipe).

(6 SERVINGS)

2 *egg whites*
Drop of lemon juice, pinch of salt
3 *cups apple purée (see* voz-dooshny pirog, *page 27)*
1 *teaspoon vanilla extract*

2 *tablespoons rum or Cognac*
1 *tablespoon grated lemon rind*
2 *envelopes unflavored gelatin*
1 *cup hot water*
1 *cup cold heavy cream*

Beat the egg whites, with a drop of lemon juice and a pinch of salt, with a wire whisk until stiff—they should hold firm peaks when the whisk is lifted from the bowl.

Add vanilla, rum or Cognac, and lemon rind to the apple purée.

Combine the whites with the apple purée in a large bowl and whisk them both together.

Dissolve the gelatin in 1 cup of hot water.

While the dissolved gelatin is cooling, whip the cold cream until it holds soft peaks.

Combine the apples and gelatin and whip the mixture until light and fluffy.

Fold in the whipped cream with a rubber spatula.

Pour the mixture into a well-chilled fancy 2-quart mold. If you forgot to chill it, rinse it out with cold water and then pour in the mixture.

Chill until it sets . . . at least 4 hours.

To serve, unmold by dipping the mold in hot water for 10 full seconds. Then put a large serving dish or plate over the top and, holding the plate and mold together firmly, turn the whole business over so that the plate is right side up and the mold is wrong side up. It should slip out of the mold easily.

MENU

Beef Pancake Pie
Fruit Purée

BEEF PANCAKE PIE
(*Blinchaty Pirog*)

A *blinchaty pirog* is a pancake pie: alternating layers of thin crêpe-like pancakes and meat and/or vegetable fillings, topped with a pancake and served piping hot with a bowl of cold sour cream.

This is by no means a light dish. As a matter of fact it's sort of heavy. But it tastes gorgeous.

The batter recipe will produce approximately six extra pancakes. Sorry. They freeze very well, so you can go ahead and make them—and then you can make *blinchaty piroshky*, or blintzes.

This recipe will make 4 very generous servings, or 6 generous servings, or as much as 8 not-so-generous servings.

(4 TO 8 SERVINGS)

It is probably easiest to prepare a *blinchaty pirog* in this order:

1. Make the fillings. This can be done way in advance—I mean several days.

2. Make the pancake batter that morning, or the day before. *Or* you can make the pancakes in advance, freeze them (stacked between layers of foil or waxed paper—so they won't stick). In this case, to thaw the crêpes, put them in a covered dish in a 300° F. oven.

3. Put together the filling and pancakes.

4. Bake the pie.

5. Eat the pie.

Beef filling:

1 *pound raw chopped beef*
1 *medium onion, minced fine*
  Butter for sautéing
½ *cup cooked rice*

3 *tablespoons sour cream (or more)*
3 *tablespoons minced dill*
2 *hard-boiled eggs, chopped*
  Salt and pepper

Sauté the beef and onions together in butter in a frying pan. When the meat is lightly browned, remove from heat and put in a bowl.

Add rice, sour cream, and dill to the meat mixture. Stir. Add a bit more sour cream if the mixture is crumbly.

When the mixture is cool, add the chopped eggs, and stir the mixture so that the ingredients are well combined.

Season with salt and pepper, and more dill if you like.

Cover the bowl and refrigerate until needed.

Mushroom filling:

> Butter for sautéing
> ½ pound mushrooms, chopped fine
> 2 scallions or 1 leek, chopped fine
> 4 ounces cream cheese, at room temperature
> Sour cream (if necessary)
> 1 tablespoon chopped dill

Sauté, in butter, in a frying pan, the mushrooms and scallions.

With a wooden spoon, cream the cream cheese in a bowl. (If the cream cheese refuses to become spreadable, add a little sour cream—about 1 tablespoon.)

When the cream cheese is spreadable, add the mushroom mixture to the cream cheese, and cream it all together as though you were making a potato-chip dip.

Add 1 tablespoon chopped dill and mix until all ingredients are thoroughly combined.

Cover the bowl and refrigerate until needed.

Batter:

> 2 cups white, all-purpose flour
> ½ teaspoon salt
> 4 large eggs
> 2 cups liquid: skimmed milk, or part water and part milk
> 4 tablespoons melted butter

This is the traditional method:

Gradually beat the eggs into the flour and salt, with a wooden spoon, in a mixing bowl. (Or do it in a mixer at low speed.)

Gradually combine all liquids, including butter, with the eggs and flour.

When the batter is smooth, pour it through a sieve into a bowl—to get all the lumps out.

Refrigerate for 2 hours at least, so that the flour particles have time to soften—and will thus yield lighter pancakes.

Here is a quick method:

Put all ingredients in a blender.

Blend at high speed for one minute until blended.

Refrigerate for 2 hours.

Assembly:

> *The batter*
> *Sour cream, 2 cups (or 16 ounces)*
> *4 ounces melted butter*

Heat a 9-inch frying pan and grease the sides and bottom lightly with butter.

Pour approximately ⅓ cup of batter into the pan, and quickly, adeptly, gracefully . . . tilt the pan all around, so the batter evenly coats the bottom and sides of the pan. Pour any batter that doesn't stick to the pan back in the batter bowl.

You might as well note exactly how much extra batter (if there was extra) this was so that you can avoid the "lip" of pancake that is formed when you pour out the excess. If you can't seem to avoid the excess, trim it off with a knife and eat it.

Cook the pancake on one side only. It is ready when the

pancake readily detaches itself from the pan, if and when the pan is shaken. Lift up a corner of the "ready" pancake, make sure it's golden brown, and remove it from the pan; to remove it, you can use your fingers or a spatula, or simply slide it out of the pan.

Put the pancake, browned side down, on a buttered cookie sheet.

Put some more batter in the frying pan, go through similar hysteria as you may have gone through in step 2, except coat only the bottom of the pan with batter. While this second pancake is cooking . . .

Brush pancake #1 with butter. Cover it with a layer of meat mixture (use about a third of the meat).

Pancake #2 should be ready now.

Put it on top of the layer of meat, browned side up. Brush it with butter. Start making pancake #3.

Put a layer of mushroom mixture on top of pancake #2 (use about half the mixture).

Pancake #3 should be ready now. Put it on top of the mushroom layer. Brush it with butter.

Start making pancake #4.

Meanwhile put on a layer of meat filling (half the remaining meat mixture). Cover meat layer with pancake #4 and brush with butter.

Start making pancake #5.

Put a layer of mushroom filling on pancake #4 (the rest of it, use it up). Cover mushroom layer with pancake #5. Brush with butter.

Start making pancake #6, but this time add extra butter and coat the sides of the pan with batter as well as the bottom.

Make the final layer of meat.

Top off the pie with pancake #6, browned side up. Brush with butter. Tuck the overhang under the pie, possibly midway down, where you can also tuck in the anti-overhang formed by the bottom pancake. Whatever you do, try to make the pie look neat.

Now, ask yourself—wasn't that fun?

Cover the pancake mass with foil and put it in the refrigerator until you are ready to heat it up and serve it.

To heat, put it in a 350° F. oven, keep it covered with foil until hot—about 15 minutes.

Serve the pancake mass with a bowl of cold sour cream with chopped dill sprinkled on top; let each person put a dollop on or beside his or her piece of pie.

To cut, slice wedges, like of an ordinary pie, using a sharp knife. If you're not a great pancake maker the pie may look raggy. Don't be dismayed, it tastes just as good ugly as it does when it's beautiful.

FRUIT PURÉE
(*Pyooray eez Sooshoneekh Frooktof*)

Compote is a very common dessert in Russia. It is, in less dignified terms, stewed fruit. In parts of the Ukraine, a very liquid compote is served as a first course—a cold fruit soup; farther north this soup is served as dessert.

Compotes may be made from fresh or dried fruits and the fruit may be left whole, cut in small pieces, or puréed.

The following fruit soup appealed to James Morgan, age three. I have a feeling it's because it tastes like first-rate baby food. If you have a little kid, keep this recipe in mind.

(4 TO 6 SERVINGS)

¾ *pound dried fruit—any kind,*   *Juice of ½ lemon*
    any combination   *Nutmeg (a few gratings)*
1 *cinnamon stick*   *Grated lemon and/or orange*
4 *cloves*   *rind to taste*
6 *cups water*   *Sour cream (optional)*
4 *tablespoons sugar (or to*
    taste)

Boil the fruit, cinnamon, cloves, and water for 20 minutes—or until the fruit is soft.

Remove the cinnamon and cloves.

Put half the fruit and liquid into the blender, and blend at high speed.

Now repeat: blend the second half of the fruit and liquid at high speed.

Return to the pot, add sugar, lemon juice, nutmeg, lemon and/or orange rinds, to taste. Bring to a boil.

Remove from heat and pour into a serving bowl, preferably glass. Serve as one might serve applesauce, with, perhaps, sour cream.

Dinners
(OBYED)

DINNER has gone through considerable evolution since the 1600's, when the emphasis was on quantity. Menus from the 1600's lacked order—it is suspected that the reason for this is that everything was served simultaneously. It is said that sometimes as many as five hundred main courses were served at the Czar's court. There were no desserts, no spices, just plain roasts and whole fish in massive quantities. An old Russian saying further illustrates the Russian perception of what is enough food: The problem with eating a goose is that it is too much for one person and too little for two people.

By the 1700's, dinner was becoming a little more refined. Wine was introduced to the menu. But again the emphasis was on quantity: Three times during the meal three different wines were served. A happy party meant that everybody was drunk.

It was only in the 1800's that dinner became a more sophisticated affair in Russia. French styles of clothing, the French language, and French food were introduced. According to Tolstoy's descriptions of dinners, the Russians adopted French elegance but they still clung to the Russian quantities.

The Russian aristocracy entertained lavishly and hired French cooks at exorbitant prices to make their dinner parties. The following excerpt from *War and Peace* describes the Russian aristocracy as it was in the mid-1800's:

"What a sauté of game au madère we are to have, my dear! I tasted it. The thousand rubles I paid for Taras [the cook] were not ill-spent. He is worth it!"

COUNT BESUKHOV

Dinner itself was huge, starting with an assortment of hors d'oeuvres called *zakoosky* and followed by a large meal with loads of different wines:

The count, followed by his guests, went into the drawing room. It was just the moment before a big dinner when the assembled guests, expecting the summons to zakuska, avoid engaging in any long conversation but think it necessary to move about and talk, in order to show that they are not impatient for their food.

When dinner was served there would be a "procession" to the dining room headed by the most important guests:

After them the other couples followed, filling the whole dining hall, and last of all the children, tutors, and governesses followed singly. The footmen began moving about, chairs scraped, the band struck up in the gallery, and the guests settled down in their places. Then the

strains of the count's household band were replaced by
the clatter of knives and forks, the voices of visitors, and
the soft steps of the footmen.

At these dinners, one end of the table was for the men, the
other for the women, and the children sat in the middle, re-
gardless of sex:

> At one end of the table sat the countess with Marya
> Dmitrievna on her right and Anna Mikhaylovna on her
> left, the other lady visitors were farther down. At the
> other end sat the count, with the hussar colonel on his left
> and Shinshin and the other male visitors on his right.
> Midway down the long table on one side sat the grown-up
> young people . . . and on the other side the children,
> tutors, and governesses.

The food was, of course, in large quantities and choices. It
was more like restaurant fare as we know it in America. Wine
was served in abundance, and it seems that even in the 1800's
the object of the party was to get drunk and happy:

> Pierre spoke little but examined the new faces, and ate
> a great deal. Of the two soups he chose turtle with savory
> patties and went on to the game without omitting a single
> dish or one of the wines. These latter the butler thrust
> mysteriously forward, wrapped in a napkin, from behind
> the next man's shoulders and whispered: "Dry Madeira"
> . . . "Hungarian" . . . or "Rhine wine" as the case might
> be. Of the four crystal glasses engraved with the count's
> monogram that stood before his plate, Pierre held out one
> at random and drank with enjoyment, gazing with ever-
> increasing amiability at the other guests.

This particular dinner that Tolstoy was describing was to celebrate Natasha's and her mother's Name Day. So this was the equivalent of a birthday party (see page 161). After dinner there was champagne and then dessert, pineapple ices at Natasha's party.

The point of this introduction to the dinner menus is to show you how the "Old Russian" concept of dinner differs greatly from the American concept. I have made the menus suitable for a normal hungry twentieth-century American family.

Hopefully, after eating a few of these Russian dinners, you will agree with a friend of mine who said, "Napoleon should have stayed for dinner!"

All the dinners will feed *at least* six people—I always like to have leftovers.

MENU

Georgian Cheese Bread

Fresh Ham Cooked
in Hay and Beer

Beets Braised
in Sour Cream

Walnut Soufflé

GEORGIAN CHEESE BREAD
(*Khadjapoory*)

In Georgia, this cheese bread is served as a dessert. However, since this book is written for non-Russians who might
feel sorely cheated if they didn't have something sweet for
dessert, I have put this in the menu as an appetizer.

The filling is made with feta cheese that can be bought in
Italian or Greek stores. In America, it can only be bought
packed in brine, so it has to soak in water for a few hours or
even overnight to reduce the saltiness to your taste. In Russia,
feta cheese can be bought without the brine, so soaking
isn't necessary there.

A yeast dough is rolled out very thin and used to enclose the
cheese filling in an unusual and fancy way. The final product

is spectacular and looks almost impossible to make. Please don't be intimidated by it. It is not difficult at all.

In the Caucasus, the *khadjapoory* is sold on the streets by vendors, in the form of little diamond-shaped open tarts. They are not half as attractive this way, nor as dramatic, but they are more convenient to serve as an hors d'oeuvre than the large bread.

NOTE:

Since the feta cheese must be soaked, it is sometimes easier to make the filling in advance, or to have the cheese ready and desalted and make the filling while the dough is rising.

Filling:

> 2 *pounds feta cheese*
> 2 *tablespoons unsalted butter*
> 2 *eggs*

Crumble the feta cheese and soak for a few hours in cold water. Taste a piece every hour and see if it has been desalted enough for you. To quicken the process, drain the cheese every ½ hour and cover with fresh water.

When the cheese is ready, first take the butter out of the refrigerator, then drain the cheese in a sieve or colander, and push it through with the back of a spoon.

Beat the eggs and mix them into the cheese.

By now the butter is a little soft. If not, break it up with your fingers or a knife and then mix it up with the cheese. When it is thoroughly combined, the filling is ready. Refrigerate until needed.

The dough:

> 2 packages dry yeast or 1 ounce compressed yeast
> 1 tablespoon sugar
> 1 cup lukewarm milk
> ¼ pound or ½ cup unsalted butter, softened
> 1 teaspoon salt
> 3½ to 4 cups all-purpose white flour, or half a
>   recipe of brioche dough (page 220)

If using compressed yeast, crumble it with the sugar and let it sit until it liquifies. If using the dry stuff, dissolve it in the lukewarm milk with the sugar.

Add the milk, yeast, sugar, butter, and salt to the flour.

With a wooden spoon, completely combine the ingredients. Beat until all the flour is absorbed into the liquid. If necessary, use your hand to mix the dough.

Knead the dough on a lightly floured board. If the dough does not stick to the board, don't bother with flouring the board. When the dough is satiny smooth and shiny, after about 10 minutes, form the dough into a ball and place in a greased bowl; turn dough over so all sides are coated. Cover the bowl with plastic wrap and a towel and let rise till double in bulk in a warm, draft-free place. This should take 45 minutes. (When the dough has risen sufficiently, a dent will remain in the dough if you poke it with your fingers.) Meanwhile . . .

If you have not made the cheese filling completely in advance, finish making it now. If you have it ready, I'm sure you can think of some way to occupy this hour.

When the dough has risen, punch it down with your fist.

Let the dough rest for 10 minutes.

Roll out the dough into a big circle, less than an ⅛-inch thick. If the dough starts getting springy, and impossible to

Bring edge of dough up over the filling to the center.

Repeat this process at regular intervals all around, pleating the dough into neat folds.

To make a knob.

The last triangular shaped flap will be larger than the rest, so twist the end around all the other points in the center.

all pleated and ready for oven.

roll, let it rest for another 10 minutes and then resume rolling.

Butter a 9-inch-round baking pan with 1-inch-high sides.

Give the dough another quick flattening, and then fold it in half, and then in fourths. Set the pointed end in the center of the pan. Then unfold the dough. (This is just a good way to center the dough.) There will be lots of dough hanging over the sides of the pan.

Put the cheese mixture into the center of the dough, mounding it somewhat higher in the center.

The next step is folding the dough. Before doing anything more, read through the instructions and pore over the diagrams so that you have a good idea of what you are going to do. I even suggest practicing folding beforehand with a round piece of paper lining a miniature pan filled with imaginary filling. Please don't be intimidated by these intimidating warnings; the folding is more difficult to explain than to actually do.

First take a section of overhang, as illustrated, and pull it over part of the cheese, toward the center of the mound. Then take another portion of overhang next to this first "fold" and bring it up to the center of the mound: it will overlap the first fold of dough, and its end will land on top of the first fold.

Continue folding by taking another fold of dough from next to the second fold, and so on, until you run out of dough.

When you reach the last fold, you will notice that it is somewhat larger than the rest. Stretch it over the remaining exposed surface of cheese, and, gathering the ends from all the other folds, form a knob in the center, using this last end to tie them all together. The bread is now folded.

Now that the dough is pleated, let the bread stand for 10 minutes before baking it. (If you want to, you can glaze the bread. Brush a beaten egg yolk on top of the bread.)

Bake at 350° F. until the crust is golden brown.

FRESH HAM COOKED IN HAY AND BEER
(Boujenina)

It is an old Ukrainian tradition, at wealthy rural estates, to prepare the ham portion of a freshly killed young pig in this manner. The ham is first brought to a boil with some hay to give it an interesting flavor and is then braised in beer.

The hay is not absolutely necessary, but try your best to get it, because it really adds a peculiar, but what I consider a delicious, flavor to the meat. Try local stables, or if your city has mounted police—ask at their stables. During Christmastime it is easier to find because it is often sold to decorate mangers. See if there are any feed and supply stores listed in the phone book.

About the beer—the closest thing to Russian *kvass*, a bread beer, would be a light beer.

1 5- to 6-pound shank portion of fresh ham with the skin on	1 carrot
	1 onion, peeled, with 6 cloves stuck into it
Piece of cheesecloth	1 stalk celery
Water	2 peppercorns
2 generous handfuls of fresh hay	1 teaspoon salt
	2 bay leaves
36 ounces light beer or kvass page 173)	

Wrap the ham in the cheesecloth and put it in a deep pot. Pour cold water into the pot until the ham is covered.

Put the hay around and over the ham, pushing it down the sides of the pot so that as much of the meat as possible is in contact with it.

Bring the water to a boil over high heat. Then turn off the flame for 2 to 3 minutes. Bring to a boil again and then reduce heat and let simmer for 10 minutes.

Remove the pot from the heat, and take out the ham; set it on a tray or large pan while you fuss with the "hay broth."

Put about 4 cups of hay broth in a bottle or a bowl. Discard the hay.

Pour the beer into the pot that was used for the hay flavoring, and add to it a peeled carrot, the cloved onion, the celery stalk, pepper, salt, and bay leaves.

Take the ham out of the cheesecloth and rinse it in warm water. Slash the skin with a knife, crossing the slashes to make a diamond-shaped design. Then put it in the pot and add about 2 cups of hay broth—so that at least half the ham is covered in liquid. The rest of the hay broth is probably not going to be needed. (If you didn't obtain hay, substitute water for hay broth.)

Simmer the ham in the pot, covered, for 2½ hours total (½ an hour per pound), giving the meat a quarter turn every ½ hour.

To serve, remove the ham from the pot and place on a carving board. If you want to, put some of the "broth" in a gravy dish and serve it with the meat. The meat is very juicy by itself, and the beer and hay flavor penetrates it well enough so that the gravy is not essential.

BEETS BRAISED IN SOUR CREAM
(*Svyokla so Smyetanoy*)

This recipe should satisfy all those people who thought Russian cooking was synonymous with sour cream and beets. It will also surprise them, because this doesn't have any of the ghastly connotations that sour cream has for many Americans. The beets color the sour cream, and the dish is a bright magenta. It's such an incredibly brilliant color that even if you hate beets, and despise sour cream, try this just to see that fantastic color!

1 *pound raw beets*	*Salt*
1 *tablespoon butter*	1 *teaspoon sugar*
1 *teaspoon lemon juice*	½ *cup sour cream*
A *little bit of water*	

Peel the beets and slice them thinly.

Melt the butter in a frying pan that has a cover. Add the beets, lemon juice, and enough water to keep the beets from burning (a few tablespoons).

Cover and simmer for about 40 minutes, or until beets are tender. Remove from heat.

Add the salt and sugar, and mix. Add the sour cream and heat the pan, but do not let the sour cream come to a boil, or it will curdle. When the cream is warm, *serve*.

Make sure the dish you serve it in shows off the beets' color. Black is very nice; so is white.

MUSHROOMS WITH SOUR CREAM *Griby so Smyetanoy*

1 *pound mushrooms, washed*
3 *tablespoons butter*
½ *teaspoon lemon juice*
 Salt and pepper
½ *cup sour cream*
 Flour (if necessary)

Slice the mushrooms, not too thin, and sauté them in butter for 10 minutes. Add lemon juice and salt and pepper. Continue cooking gently, stir carefully.

Add sour cream, and continue cooking over tiny flame, very low heat, until the sour cream is heated through. If it comes to a boil, the sour cream will curdle.

The sauce should be the consistency of thick cream. If it's too thin, add a bit of flour; if it's too thick, add a bit of water.

To make a variation on a variation, try mushrooms au gratin: Sprinkle the top of the mushrooms with grated cheese. Brown under a broiler or in an oven.

WALNUT SOUFFLÉ
(*Oryekhovoye Souffé*)

½ *pound walnuts*
½ *cup sugar*
½ *cup cream*
5 *eggs, separated, at room temperature*
¼ *teaspoon lemon juice*
Pinch of salt

Grind the walnuts in a nut grinder or blender.

Combine the sugar, cream, and egg yolks in an unheated saucepan—a whisk is good for this, although the mixture should be "stirred," not "beaten."

Add the walnuts to the saucepan and heat over a small flame, stirring constantly. Do not let it boil.

When the mixture is quite thick and golden brown—this takes about 5 to 7 minutes—remove from heat and set aside until about ½ hour before you want to serve the soufflé.

Now that it is ½ hour before dessert, preheat the oven to 350° F. Beat the egg whites, with ¼ teaspoon lemon juice and a pinch of salt until they hold peaks when the beater is lifted from the bowl, but are still moist, not dry as for meringues.

With a fork, or a chopstick, stir the walnut mixture so that it is somewhat broken up, but not one lump.

Butter a soufflé dish—a round, flat-bottomed, high-walled dish.

Fold half of the egg whites into the walnut mixture with a rubber spatula. Do this with some care—try not to knock all the air out of the whites. Then fold in the second half.

When the egg whites and walnuts are well combined, pour into the soufflé dish and bake for ½ hour at 350° F. or until the soufflé has doubled in bulk and the top is browned and beginning to crack.

Serve immediately: Take a spoon and cut out mock wedges.

MENU

Cold Beer Soup
Caucasian Roast Lamb
Pilaf with Almonds
and Dried Fruit
Czar's Icebox Cake

COLD BEER SOUP (IRINA-STYLE)
(*Okroshka*)

Okroshka is a cold soup—refreshing, unusual, and ideal for a hot summer day.

The base of the soup is *kvass*, Russian bread beer, which tastes like a milk beer. Some people might shy away from making the beer from scratch. But let me assure you, it is not so difficult to make. As a matter of fact, it isn't difficult at all—it's just a question of setting aside the time. When I make it I start it in the evening and then do the next step in the morning; later that evening I bottle it. From that point on it's just a question of waiting for the *kvass* to mature. If you still are not excited by the idea of making your very own, delicious *kvass*, however, substitute soda water, or a dry champagne.

This is a do-it-yourself soup. The *kvass* is served in a bottle.

Then there are four bowls of goodies to put in your soup bowl. The *kvass* is then poured over your pile of goodies, and your soup is ready.

1 quart kvass *(see page 173)*

Bowl 1:

5 small cucumbers, peeled and grated
2 hard-boiled eggs, chopped
4 new potatoes or 2 large potatoes, boiled and mashed

Combine the above ingredients, prepared as indicated.

Bowl 2:

Scallion greens
Salt and pepper

Coarsely chop the scallion greens. Then sprinkle with salt and pepper, and hammer them so that they're very flat. This makes the scallion juice flavor the soup as soon as it is put in.

Bowl 3:

Precooked frankfurters and/or sausages, cut into bite-sized rounds

Bowl 4:

Chopped fresh dill

To serve *okroshka*, put the bowls out on a table, with a serving spoon in each, and the *kvass*, well chilled in its bottle or in a pitcher. Each person will help him/herself to the goodies from the bowl, in whatever proportion he/she wants, and then pour *kvass* over it.

CAUCASIAN ROAST LAMB
(*Jarenaya Baranina po Kavkasky*)

There is no way this dish can be a flop unless, of course, you burn the meat or don't get all the spices. Roast lamb is delicious by itself and there is no heavy sauce to mask its natural flavor.

The meat is coated with yogurt and herbs and then roasted. The use of yogurt and the pilaf, which are traditionally served with the lamb, shows the influence of the Greeks and Turks on the other side of the mountains.

The buttermilk marinade is very important because it tenderizes the meat. This is the old-fashioned way to tenderize meat without using all the dubious chemicals available today. The bacteria that sours the milk breaks down the meat tissues, and so tenderizes it.

3½ to 4 pounds boned shoulder of lamb, tied in a cushion shape (Ask your butcher to prepare it for you.)
2 cloves garlic, slivered
1 quart buttermilk
¼ cup yogurt
1 teaspoon ground coriander seed
½ teaspoon ground cumin
1 teaspoon marjoram
½ teaspoon chopped dill
¼ teaspoon salt
¼ teaspoon freshly ground black pepper
¼ cup vegetable oil (for basting)

The day before:

Cut two cloves of garlic into slivers.

Pierce the lamb with the point of a sharp knife and stud it

with a sliver of garlic. Repeat this all over the surface of the meat.

Put the meat in a heavy-duty plastic bag or in a deep bowl with a cover, and pour 1 quart of buttermilk over it. Let it marinate in the refrigerator for 24 to 36 hours.

The day of the meal:

After marinating the lamb, discard the buttermilk and pat the lamb dry with paper towels.

Make the sauce by mixing the yogurt and spices, and spread it over the lamb. Put the lamb in a roasting pan.

Spoon the oil over the lamb and roast in a 375° F. oven for 1½ to 1¾ hours or until a meat thermometer registers 150° F.

Remove the strings, and carve the lamb at the table.

PILAF WITH ALMONDS AND DRIED FRUIT
(*Plov*)

Pilaf is designed to be cooked over an open fire. The cooking is begun over very high heat, then the pilaf bakes more slowly as the open fire dies down. The following method is the modern stove imitation.

3 tablespoons vegetable oil

1 cup raw rice

2 cups chicken stock (either canned, dehydrated, or fresh)

½ cup raisins (Yellow raisins make it more attractive.)

½ cup chopped prunes, peaches, or apricots

½ cup or 2¼ ounces slivered almonds

Green part of 3 scallions, sliced

In the casserole heat the oil and fry the rice gently until the grains turn transparent, just before they begin to brown.

Pour on the stock, bring to a boil, and then cover the pot and bake in a 350° F. oven for 15 minutes.

Stir in the fruit, nuts, and scallions. Continue baking for 5 minutes, until the rice is tender and the liquid is absorbed.

Let stand 10 minutes before removing the cover and stirring the rice.

Serve in a bowl.

CZAR'S ICEBOX CAKE
(*Shokoladnaya Sharlotka*)

This recipe was given to me by Mrs. Ralph Bogorad—it is a Bogorad family heirloom.

Whipped cream and stiffly beaten egg whites are folded into melted chocolate and egg yolks. This mixture is poured into a spring-form pan that has been lined with split ladyfingers. The dessert is refrigerated for about 4 hours so that the custard sets. It is then unmolded, served, and eaten up.

My theory is that Czar's icebox cake is the great-grandchild of the peasant apple *sharlotka* (see pages 38–40).

First came apple *sharlotka*: a pudding made from alternating layers of puréed apples and black-bread crumbs. A refinement on apple *sharlotka* was to neatly line the *charlotte* mold with thin slices of bread and then pour in the puréed apples (which now needed to be thickened with egg yolks—that is more of a custardy filling). Then French cooks were imported by Russian nobility. The French cooks substituted thin slices of *génoise* or sponge cake for the thin slices of bread in the *sharlotka*. Having made this refinement, the French cooks began to experiment with the fillings. This must be where the French *charlotte russe* (a dessert like Czar's icebox cake but filled with a fruit custard—e.g., raspberry) and the French classic *charlotte Malakoff* (a *charlotte* filled with almond cream) must have originated.

Whether Czar's icebox cake is a variation of *charlotte russe* or whether *charlotte russe* is a variation of Czar's icebox cake, and whether either recipe is French or Russian, matters very little, since this is one hell of a smashing dessert.

(10 TO 12 SERVINGS)

24 ladyfinger halves (type of sponge cake sold commercially)
4 squares unsweetened chocolate
2 tablespoons hot water
½ cup sugar
4 eggs, separated

1 teaspoon vanilla extract
Pinch of salt
Pinch of cream of tartar
1 cup well-chilled heavy cream (Put it in the freezer for 15 minutes before using it.)

Split the ladyfingers in half lengthwise. Trim 24 of the ladyfinger halves as shown in the diagram. Place these trimmed halves, side by side, curved sides down, on the bottom of a 2-quart *charlotte* mold or an 8-inch spring-form pan, with the tapered ends meeting in the center. Stand the remaining, untapered, ladyfingers, curved side out, side by side around the inside of the mold, avoiding, if you can, any gaps between them. (See diagram.)

Melt the chocolate in a double boiler with the hot water. Add all but 2 tablespoons of the sugar and stir with a wooden spoon until the sugar is completely dissolved and the mixture is well blended.

Remove the mixture from over the boiling water and add

Czar's Ice Box Cake

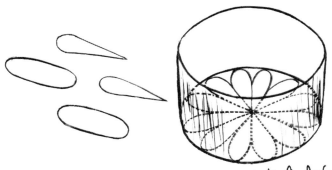

cut ladyfingers
to fit bottom of mold

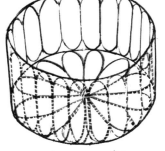

line side of mold
with vertical ladyfingers

unmolded

the egg yolks one at a time, beating thoroughly after each addition.

Replace the pan over the boiling water and cook, constantly stirring, for 10 minutes. Then remove it again and add the vanilla extract. Mix. Then place the pan in a bowl of ice water, and stir until the mixture thickens.

Beat the egg whites with a pinch of salt, 2 tablespoons sugar, and cream of tartar, using a wire whisk, until they are light and airy and will hold firm peaks when the beater is lifted from the bowl.

Fold the egg whites into the still-warm chocolate mixture, using a rubber spatula, taking care not to beat all the air out of the egg whites while you are combining the chocolate and whites.

Whip the cream until it holds firm peaks when the beater is lifted from the bowl and then fold into the cooled chocolate mixture, until well combined.

Transfer the chocolate mixture to the ladyfinger-lined *charlotte* mold or spring-form pan. Smooth the top with a spatula. Cover with plastic wrap and refrigerate for 4 to 5 hours, or until the custard has set.

To serve, invert a flat serving plate on top of the *charlotte* mold or spring-form pan and, grasping the plate and mold firmly together, turn them over. Gently remove the mold or pan by wiggling it slightly until the pudding slides out. If using a spring-form pan, open the side, of course, and it will come out easily—but be cautious.

MENU

Dried Mushroom Soup

String Beans
with Walnut Sauce

Pressed Chicken
with Garlic Sauce

Pancake Pie
with Raisins and Walnuts

DRIED MUSHROOM SOUP
(*Gribnoi*)

Gribnoi is usually eaten during the winter, when fresh vegetables are unobtainable, and during Lent, when meat is forbidden. Dried mushrooms were sold in Moscow at the mushroom fair during Lent. They were sold on strings, similar to daisy chains. The closest thing to Russian dried mushrooms are the dried black mushrooms sold in Chinese food stores. You can dry your own (see page 172) but the problem is that you will not be using the right variety of mushrooms.

This soup has a fantastic aroma and is best eaten freshly made.

6 ounces dried black mush-
    rooms—Chinese type
7 cups water
1 large onion, chopped
¼ pound butter (1 stick)
3 cups water

1¼ cups beef bouillon
4 potatoes, peeled and cut
    into little cubes
Salt and pepper to taste
A dollop sour cream

Soak the mushrooms in 4 cups of water for 2 hours—until soft enough to slice. Then drain them and wash under running water. Slice them.

Chop the onion, and brown it in 2 tablespoons of the butter.

Brown mushrooms in another 2 tablespoons of the butter.

Boil 3 cups of water and 1¼ cups of bouillon together. Add the mushrooms and onions.

Boil, partially covered, for 10 minutes. Add the potatoes and the remainder of the butter. Simmer until the potatoes are soft but not mushy. Salt and pepper the soup. Add more water if there is too much vegetable and no broth.

Serve with a tablespoon of sour cream on each serving.

STRING BEANS WITH WALNUT SAUCE
(*Boboviye Stroochky v Oryekhovom Sosye*)

Walnut sauce is very exotic tasting. The coriander and paprika make it spicy but not painful to the palate. This is a typical Caucasian sauce: the Caucasians grow a lot of nuts and coriander and so they throw them both into everything.

Attention: There is no way you can prepare the walnut sauce without coriander leaves. Grow it! Or find an Italian or Chinese grocery store and ask for *cilantro*. The flavor is exquisite. My Russian teacher traveled for an hour and a half to buy thirty-five cents worth. If it is virtually impossible to obtain, substitute Italian flat-leaf parsley, but feel very guilty about it.

4 ounces walnuts
¼ cup chopped onion
¼ cup chopped fresh coriander (or, if necessary, Italian flat-leaf parsley)

1½ teaspoons salt
2 teaspoons paprika
Freshly ground black pepper to taste
¼ cup red wine vinegar
1 pounds string beans

Either pound all the ingredients, except the vinegar, in a mortar or put *all* ingredients in a blender.

If using a mortar and pestle, after the ingredients are mashed into a paste combine with the vinegar.

Pour the sauce over boiled string beans at room temperature.

PRESSED CHICKEN
(*Tabaka*)

This Georgian method of preparing chicken consists of removing the back and breast bones of the bird, then flattening out the chicken, bringing the legs underneath the breast. It is then fried under a weight so the bird browns and cooks very quickly, retaining this flat shape. The meat stays very juicy with this method of cooking, and the skin is crisp and a deep golden brown.

It is served with a garlic sauce.

In the Soviet Union, *tabaka* is served with a skewer of *shashlyk*, and two different sauces. The garlic sauce is for the *tabaka*, and the *tkemali* sauce, a pungent sauce made from prunes, is for the *shashlyk*. Here, *tabaka* alone is plenty for dinner, if a normal two-pound chicken is shared between two people. In Russia they have tiny chickens, similar to our Rock Cornish hens, but I recommend using two-pound chickens because they stay moister and taste better than Rock Cornish hens.

3 *2¼- to 2½-pound fryers or*
6 *1- to 1¼-pound Rock Cornish hens*
   (The larger chickens are less trouble, but the small ones are more traditional.)
   Salt
3 *tablespoons sour cream*
6 *tablespoons clarified butter*

Pat the chickens dry with a paper towel.

Remove the backbone and tail. Remove the breast bone without cutting through the skin. Follow detailed instructions below for these operations, referring to the illustrations also:

Using a kitchen shears or a sharp boning knife, cut along one side of the backbone, starting from the tail end, keeping as close to the bone as possible. Cut all the way through to the ex-neck.

Make a similar second cut along the other side of the backbone, all the way through to the other side of the ex-neck. When you have completed this second cut, you will notice that the backbone and the tail (one piece) are no longer attached to the chicken. Take this back-and-tail piece and put it in a small pot with 1½ cups water, a piece of onion studded with 2 cloves, ½ peeled carrot, a pinch of salt and 3 whole peppercorns. Let this simmer on the stove. (This mixture will become the chicken-stock base for the garlic sauce to be served with the *tabaka*.)

Pressed Chicken

Tabaka

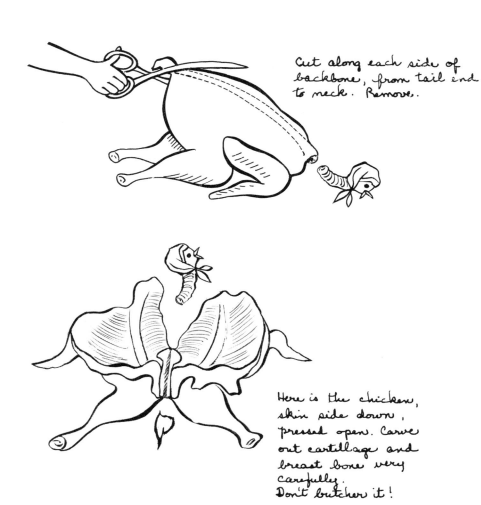

Cut along each side of
backbone, from tail end
to neck. Remove.

Here is the chicken,
skin side down,
pressed open. Carve
out cartilage and
breast bone very
carefully.
Don't butcher it!

Turn chicken over,
skin side up.
With mallet, pound
to flatten curved ribs.

make a slit in each breast.

Tuck legs under breast
and pull each drumstick
knob through.

After that second cut, the chicken will be lying on her belly, and her inner cavity should be completely exposed by the now-open back. Looking at the chicken from the tail end, you will see a white feather-shaped piece of cartilage that leads up to the breastbone. Cut this yoke cartilage with your boning knife in a downward slit so that you are releasing the tension between the 2 halves of the yoke. Flatten the breast out with your hand.

Now carve out the white-feather cartilage with the boning knife. Take care not to mutilate the muscle or skin of the chicken. It helps to use your fingers to separate the muscle from the cartilage. Continue carving along the cartilage and cut out the breastbone and yoke as well while you're in the neighborhood.

The worst is over now; you can throw out the cartilage and add the breastbone to the chicken stock that should be simmering in its little pot on the stove.

Now turn over the chicken so she is breast side up. Give each leg a good strong twist until you hear the joint crack. The legs will now move freely in their sockets, although they are still attached to the chicken.

Now twist a leg under and back so that the knob of the leg is under the lower part of the breast. Make a slit with the boning knife. Poke the knob of the bent-back chicken leg through the slit. Repeat with the other leg.

Bend the wing tips under the chicken so that the wings don't stick up funny.

With a wooden mallet or a heavy frying pan, give the chicken 4 good whacks—one for each wing area and one for each leg area—so that the chicken lies flat.

Put it aside, pick up the next bird, and repeat the process until you run out of chickens.

Sprinkle the pressed chickens liberally with salt. Then, with a pastry brush or a spoon, spread ½ tablespoon of sour cream on the fleshy underside of the chicken. It is now ready for frying.

Get two heavy skillets, preferably iron. If using squab, cook 2 at a time—this all depends on your skillet size. A 10- to 12-inch size is best. Find some heavy weights—a brick, a smaller, heavy skillet, a piece of marble—you will put these weights in one pan.

In the other, heat under a high flame 2 tablespoons clarified butter until brown.

Place flattened chicken skin side down in the pan. Put pan with weights on top and reduce heat to medium low so the bird will brown, not burn.

Cook for 10 minutes and, when golden brown, turn the chicken, spread ½ tablespoon of sour cream on the deep golden brown, cooked side, and cover with the weighted pan again.

Cook another 10 minutes and remove from the skillet. Put the chicken, skin side up, on an oven-proof platter and place in the oven. Set it at 250° F. so it will stay warm while you prepare the rest.

Repeat this process until you are out of chickens.

Serve with a bowl of garlic sauce.

If serving squab give one to each person. If serving the fryers, show them uncut to the company, then cut them in half. The only possible impediment to the cutting is the wishbone.

GARLIC SAUCE
(*Chesnochny Sos*)

This sauce keeps the chicken moist, besides adding a nice garlic flavor.

1½ *cups chicken stock*
6 *cloves garlic, peeled*
½ *teaspoon salt*
1 *tablespoon chopped parsley*

To make the chicken stock, put the left-over wing tips and other bones from the pressed chicken in a pot with just enough water to cover them, some salt and pepper, a carrot, bay leaf, a piece of celery, a slice of onion, etc. Let simmer, covered, for about ½ hour, or until the water is flavored by the chicken stock. Measure out 1½ cups of stock and set it aside.

Smash each clove of garlic with the flat side of a knife. Sprinkle the smashed garlic with the ½ teaspoon of salt and then chop the garlic until it is very fine. The salt makes it easier to chop.

Put the chopped garlic into the chicken stock, along with the tablespoon of chopped parsley. Heat up the sauce before serving.

Serve in a gravy boat.

PANCAKE PIE WITH RAISINS AND WALNUTS
(*Blinchaty Pirog s Eezyoomom ee Oryekhamy*)

Alternating layers of crêpes and a honey, raisin, and nut filling, served piping hot right from the oven, make a spectacular dessert. It tastes like *baklava*, although it is entirely different. I suppose what I really mean is that if you like *baklava*, you will like this *blinchaty pirog*. It is made in the same way as the *blinchaty pirog* made with meat (see page 51).

It can be made way in advance, and even frozen. All you have to do is defrost it and then shove it in the oven before serving.

By the way, this is a Georgian preparation.

Half a batch of pancake batter (see blinchaty pirog, *page 51)*

Filling:

6 *ounces coarsely chopped walnuts*
2 *cups raisins—half golden and half dark*
⅜ *pound unsalted butter (1½ sticks)*
1 *cup sugar*
¼ *cup honey*

Make the batter and set aside.

Mix the nuts and raisins together in a bowl.

Melt and clarify the butter. Then add the sugar to the butter and heat the pot. Let the sugar and butter bubble together until the sugar is completely dissolved, about 10 minutes.

Mix the honey, sugar, butter, nuts, and raisins together in the bowl. Set aside or refrigerate until ready to put the pie together.

Assembly:

Make it almost the same way as the other *blinchaty pirog,* *except* that the filling will not spread over the pancakes. Instead, dot the pancakes with filling so that there will be enough to use 6 pancakes, 9 inches in diameter.

Sprinkle the top of the pie with powered sugar just before serving.

Serve cut in wedges—there is no accompaniment for this pie except a strong cup of Turkish coffee.

MENU

Sorrel Soup with Eggs
Salmon Pie
Health Salad Kiev Style
Almond and Glazed
Fruit Ice Cream

SORREL SOUP WITH EGGS
(*Shchav*)

(FROM ANNA MARKIEVICH)

This is a terriffic cold summer soup. It is very easy to prepare. It is made of sour grass—or sorrel leaves—or what is sometimes simply known as *shchav*.

This is also served with little cubes of beef: First brown the cubes in butter, then boil them in water or with the *shchav* broth when you cook the sour grass.

A soup that tastes similar to this but is easier to make is Azerbaijan yogurt soup; the recipe follows this one.

2 *pounds fresh sorrel leaves (sour grass), washed and stemmed (or*
    1 large jar prepared shchav *with eggs)*
3 *peeled and diced cucumbers*
4 *scallions, finely chopped (use green and white parts)*

2 *beaten eggs*
1 *pint (16 ounces) sour cream*
   Salt and pepper to taste

If using fresh sorrel, wash and stem the leaves, then cover with boiling water and add salt to taste. Simmer for 10 minutes or until leaves are tender.

Strain and reserve liquid. Then chop the leaves fine and return to the liquid. So far, you have made the broth, the equivalent—except, of course, in an aesthetic sense—of the commercial *shchav*.

Add the diced cucumbers, minced scallions, and the two beaten eggs. Mix completely.

Add the sour cream. Mix. Then add salt and pepper to taste —heavy on the pepper.

Serve chilled, in bowls.

AZERBAIJAN YOGURT SOUP
(*Yoogurtny Soop*)

This is a good summer soup—very refreshing.

2 *cups yogurt*
2 *cups water*
1 *large cucumber, or 2 small pickling variety cucumbers, peeled and chopped*
4 *to 5 tablespoons chopped scallions, green and white parts*

Chopped fresh dill
2 *teaspoons sugar*
   Salt and pepper to taste
   Optional: ¾ pound ½-inch cubes of beef, fried in butter until cooked and browned

Mix all ingredients, prepared as indicated.
Chill before serving.

SALMON PIE
(*Kulebyaka*)

Kulebyaka is a meat or fish pie, traditionally made in an oblong shape. The secretary in Anton Chekhov's story "The Siren" describes rather sensuously the experience of eating this Russian dish:

> "The Kulebyaka must make your mouth water, it should be voluptuous, so to say, in all its glory. As you cut yourself a piece of it, you wink at it, and, your heart overflowing with delight, you let your fingers pass over it. . . . Then you start eating it, and the butter drips like large tears, and the stuffing is succulent, luscious, there are eggs in it . . . and onions . . . Yes, yes, you eat two pieces of Kulebyaka at once . . . but the third piece you reserve for the soup . . ."

The best way to approach the construction of a *kulebyaka* is in stages:

1. First choose the dough. Puff pastry or a *brioche* dough is traditional. The puff pastry makes a buttery, flaky crust; it takes 10 minutes to prepare, and can survive 3 weeks of refrigeration. The *brioche* dough makes a rich egg crust, perhaps more of a bread—delicious. *Brioche* dough takes several hours to prepare, because it's a yeast dough and requires rising time; it also lasts only 3 days in the refrigerator.

2. Make the dough and refrigerate it.

3. Prepare the salmon and mushrooms.

4. Prepare the rice and eggs. This must be done *after* the salmon because the rice is cooked in the fish stock.

5. Just before assembling the *kulebyaka,* prepare the cream sauce.

6. Assemble the *kulebyaka.*

Puff-pastry dough:
Brioche *dough:*

The recipes for these doughs can be found on pages 219 to 222.

Salmon and mushroom filling:

5 *cups water*	½ *cup finely minced scallions*
5 *cloves*	*or onions*
1 *small onion, peeled*	3 *tablespoons butter*
1 *small carrot, peeled*	½ *pound mushrooms, finely*
5 *peppercorns*	*chopped*
½ *lemon*	1 *cup dry white wine*
1 *tablespoon salt*	½ *cup chopped dill*
1½ *pounds fresh salmon, in 1*	*Juice of 1 small lemon*
piece	*Salt and pepper*

PART 1:

In a 3-quart pot boil 5 cups of water, an onion with the 5 cloves stuck in it, a carrot, 5 peppercorns, half a lemon, and 1 tablespoon of salt. Boil for 10 minutes.

Add the salmon to the boiling water. Add more water, if necessary, to cover it.

Cover and simmer over low heat for 15 to 20 minutes—until fish flakes easily with a fork. Remove the fish and let it cool in a bowl.

Strain and save the fish stock for the rice and egg filling and the cream sauce.

PART 2:

Sauté the chopped scallions or onions in 2 tablespoons of butter. Reserve.

Sauté the chopped mushrooms in 1 tablespoon of butter.

Stir the mushrooms and 1 cup of white wine into the chopped scallions and bring to a boil to reduce the liquid by half.

Stir in the salmon and the dill.

Season with the juice of 1 small lemon and with salt and pepper.

Refrigerate until needed.

Rice and egg filling:

> *2 tablespoons butter*
> *1 cup raw white rice*
> *3 cups fish stock*
> *3 hard-boiled eggs, peeled and chopped*
> *Salt and pepper*

In a 2-quart saucepan melt the butter and stir in the rice; cook for a few minutes over low heat until the rice grains are milky.

Pour in the fish stock and bring to a boil. Stir lightly and cover pan; let simmer for 20 minutes until the rice has absorbed the fish stock.

With a fork, fluff the rice lightly. Then add the chopped eggs and season with salt and pepper.

Medium cream sauce:

> *2 cups liquid (use leftover fish stock and, if necessary, add milk to make 2 cups)*
> *2 tablespoons butter*
> *3½ tablespoons flour*
> *Salt and pepper*

Boil the fish stock.

Meanwhile heat the butter in a saucepan (1½ quart), add flour, and combine with butter, using a whisk.

Keep stirring the butter and flour over the heat until it bubbles. (This is a "white roux.")

Remove from heat, and as soon as it stops bubbling stir in the hot fish stock, gradually, using a whisk.

Set saucepan over moderate heat and stir with the whisk until the sauce comes to a boil.

Boil for 1 minute, stirring constantly until thick. Season with salt and pepper.

Assembly:

1 egg yolk, 1 tablespoon cream, butter

Roll the dough out on a large (2 feet long) piece of foil. Roll it into a large rectangle, about 14 x 16 inches, and somewhat less than ¼ inch thick.

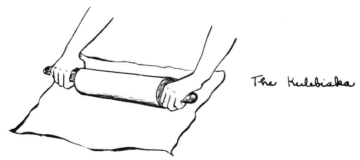

The Kulebiaka

Trim the edges of the rectangle, to make even sides (save the scraps; if using puff pastry, do not bunch up these scraps but leave them flat; they will be used for decorating the finished *kulebyaka*). To do this, use a single-edge razor blade, or a pastry wheel.

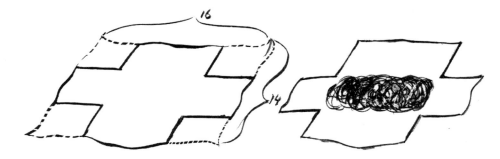

Cut a small rectangle out of each corner as in the diagram.

Put half the rice and egg filling in the center third of the dough rectangle. Make the layer long and narrow. Place half the salmon mixture on top of the rice, and spoon some of the cream sauce over the salmon (somewhat less than half).

Put the rest of the rice on top of the layer of salmon and sauce. Put the rest of the salmon on top.

Pour some more cream sauce on top of the salmon. (There is no obligation to use all the cream sauce—use your judgment.)

Bring the short sides of dough over the ends of the filling.

Brush the long edges of dough with beaten egg yolk and fold over the filling. You may have to put the filling into a flatter or a taller mound so the dough can fit over it.

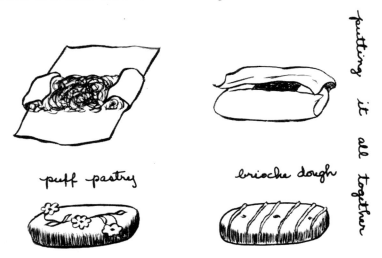

puff pastry

brioche dough

putting it all together

Wrap the *kulebyaka* in the foil. Carefully turn it over onto a cookie sheet. Use other people, spatulas, etc., for turning it over without breaking it.

The *kulebyaka* should have three round holes cut out along the top to let steam escape.

With the scraps of dough, leaf shapes or flowers can be cut out and glued onto the top of the *kulebyaka* with egg yolk, in some sort of design.

Brush the *kulebyaka* with an egg yolk mixed with a tablespoon of cream.

Bake in an oven, preheated to 450° F., for 10 minutes. Then reduce the heat to 375° F. and cook until golden brown.

Serve with a sauceboat of melted butter.

NOTE:

When using brioche dough, long strips of dough are used to indicate portions.

HEALTH SALAD KIEV STYLE
(*Zdorovie Salat po Kievskie*)

This is a fresh salad, with apples and carrots and tomatoes on a bed of lettuce, with sour cream dressing. It is one of those great, refreshing salads that is a good preparation for dessert.

(6 TO 8 SERVINGS)

1 *large cucumber, peeled*	⅔ *cup sour cream*
2 *raw carrots, peeled*	1 *teaspoon lemon juice*
2 *apples, washed*	½ *tablespoon sugar*
1 *small head Romaine lettuce*	*Salt and pepper to taste*
2 *small tomatoes*	

Cut the cucumber, carrots, and apples into short sticks—bite size, but big enough to be eaten with a fork.

Select 6 to 8 leaves of lettuce, 1 per person, and tear into 3 or 4 pieces each. Lay these lettuce pieces on the bottom of a serving dish.

Arrange the cucumber, carrot, and apple sticks on top of the lettuce.

Cut the tomatoes into wedges; again make them small enough to fit in your mouth. Arrange them on top of the cucumbers, carrots, and apples.

Mix sour cream and lemon juice with sugar, salt, and pepper, and pour over the vegetables.

Serve immediately.

ALMOND AND GLAZED FRUIT
ICE CREAM
(*Plombir*)

This is an elegant Russian ice cream. It is made of whipped sweet cream mixed with ground almonds and glazed fruits, frozen in a simple mold. It is served unmolded garnished with toasted, sliced almonds and grenadine. It's simple to prepare —taking about 1 hour altogether—and can be kept in the freezer for weeks.

1½ *cups chopped glazed mixed fruit (the type used for fruit cakes)*
2 *teaspoons vanilla extract*
1 *teaspoon almond extract*
3 *cups heavy cream, chilled*
½ *cup confectioner's sugar*
¼ *pound blanched, toasted almonds pulverized in a mortar, nut grinder, or blender*

GARNISH: *Grenadine*
         ⅛ pound sliced, toasted almonds

Soaked the glazed fruit in the vanilla and almond extracts.

In a large chilled bowl beat the heavy cream with a whisk, rotary beater, or electric beater. (Either chill the bowl in the refrigerator or set it in a larger bowl containing ice.) Beat until cream starts to get thick; then beat in confectioner's sugar, gradually, until it is thoroughly combined with the cream. Continue beating until the cream is thick and holds fairly firm peaks when the beater is lifted out of the bowl.

Fold into the cream, with a rubber spatula, the ground almonds and the glazed fruit. Do not stir; be gentle and try not to knock the air out of the whipped cream. When the ingredients are well combined . . .

Pour contents into a 1½-quart *charlotte* mold or soufflé dish. Cover with foil or plastic wrap and freeze it for at least 4 or 5 hours—until firm. It can last indefinitely in the freezer—like ordinary ice cream.

To serve, unmold by dipping the bottom of the mold in hot water for 15 seconds and then running a knife along the inside edge of the mold.

Invert a plate and place on top of the mold. Then, holding the plate and mold firmly, turn them over. The *plombir* should slide out easily. If it doesn't come out, don't panic—just dip the bottom of the mold in hot water again and continue.

Garnish: Pour grenadine syrup on the center of the top of the mound of ice cream. It will gradually spread and drip down the sides of the cream, giving it a bird cage appearance.

Cover the top with sliced almonds.

To cut wedges, first dip the serving knife in hot water; the ice cream is easier to cut with a sharp knife.

MENU

Cold Apple Soup

Carrot Pancakes

Pork Chops with

Cherry or Prune Sauce

Poppy Seed Roll

COLD APPLE SOUP
(*Kholodny Yablochny Soop*)

This is a delicious thick fruit soup served ice cold with vanilla rusks. It is made from puréed apples, spices, and dry red wine.

Originally from Poland, which was once part of Russia, cold fruit soups are common in the Baltic and Lithuanian states of the Soviet Union. The resemblance of *yablochny soop* to Scandinavian fruit soup is not your imagination: Scandinavia is just across the Baltic Sea from the Baltic states.

6 *large eating apples*	1 *teaspoon ground cinnamon*
½ *lemon*	½ *teaspoon ground cloves*
1 *teaspoon vanilla extract*	2 *cups water*
½ *cup sugar*	1 *cup dry red wine*

Peel, core, and coarsely chop the apples.

Squeeze the juice of half a lemon over the chopped apples. Grate the rind.

Put vanilla, sugar, cinnamon, the grated lemon rind, cloves, apples, and 2 cups of water in a pot and partly cover it.

Bring to a boil and then reduce heat at once and simmer for 20 minutes, stirring occasionally.

When the apples are soft and mushy add the wine, stir, and chill.

Serve ice cold; preferably in chilled bowls.

BLUEBERRY SOUP
(Chernichny Soop)

1 *pint blueberries*
¼ *cup sugar*
1 *cinnamon stick*
2 *cups water*
1 *lemon, quartered*
   Sour cream (optional)

Put the blueberries, sugar, and cinnamon stick in a pot with the water. Squeeze the lemon quarters into the pot. Throw quarters into the pot. Bring to a boil.

Simmer for 15 minutes, and then let the soup cool.

Without removing lemon remains or cinnamon, put in a blender or through a food mill. Chill.

Serve cold, with a dollop of sour cream in each bowl.

CARROT PANCAKES
(*Kotlety eez Markovky*)

These are small patties of shredded carrots cooked with
butter and semolina, then fried and served with a sour cream
sauce. This is a typical Baltic preparation. They make potato
patties, turnip patties, and cabbage patties in a similar way.

2½ *pounds carrots*   ½ *cup farina or semolina*
  3 *tablespoons butter*   3 *eggs, separated (lightly beat*
  ⅔ *cup hot milk*   *the yolks and white)*
  1 *teaspoon sugar*   *Bread crumbs*
    Salt

Peel and grate the carrots. Place them in a cooking pot and
add 1 tablespoon of the butter, all the milk, and the sugar,
plus a dash of salt.

Cover with a lid and cook over a low flame, stirring often.
Cook until tender—about 15 to 20 minutes.

Add the farina or semolina gradually, stirring all the time.
Continue cooking, covered, for 8 to 10 minutes.

Remove the carrots from the fire and let them cool for 3
minutes.

Add 3 egg yolks, mixing thoroughly. Then cool or refrigerate
until needed.

Form small patties—2 to 2½ inches in diameter. Brush
them with lightly beaten egg white and roll in bread crumbs.

Fry the patties in butter on both sides until browned.

PORK CHOPS WITH CHERRY SAUCE OR PRUNE SAUCE

The pork chops are breaded and fried in sour cream (as bizarre as this may sound, this is one of the best ways to cook pork chops), and served with cherry sauce. The idea of serving fruit with meat was introduced by Peter the Great in the early 1700's. He was determined to Westernize or modernize Russia by opening the "windows to the west." Besides bringing back coffee from Holland, and introducing new hair styles, new clothing, a new calendar, printing presses, and a school system, and being the first monarch in Russia to invite women to dine with him at his dinner table, Peter the Great made a contribution to Russian cookery, and pork with fresh cherries is no doubt an offshoot of this project for mass reform.

PORK CHOPS
(*Cvinniye Otbivniye*)

6 *loin pork chops*, 1½ *inches thick*
  Flour
1 *beaten egg*
  Bread crumbs
  Butter
½ *cup sour cream*

Pat the chops dry with paper towel, and slash the fat around the edges to keep it from curling when cooking.

Dip the chops in flour and brush them with lightly beaten egg. Roll them in bread crumbs.

Brown the chops in a frying pan, in butter, quickly on both sides.

Remove the chops, drain off the fat, and put sour cream in the pan. Replace the chops, and simmer, covered, for 20 minutes.

Serve with cherry or prune sauce (below) poured over the chops.

CHERRY OR PRUNE SAUCE
(*Sos eez Chernyeshen ily Sliv*)

1 1-*pound jar whole unpitted dark sweet cherries in a heavy syrup*
     or a 1-pound jar stewed prunes
  Grated peel of ½ orange
½ *teaspoon ground cinnamon*
¼ *teaspoon ground cloves*
½ *cup port wine*

NOTE:
Save the syrup from the cherries.

Pit the cherries and *save the pits* (for flavoring vodka).

Put the cherries in a pot with the heavy syrup and bring to a boil. Take off heat after 2 minutes of boiling and drain the cherries, reserving the syrup.

Put them in a blender and then push them through a sieve with the back of a wooden spoon.

Add the grated orange peel, cinnamon, and cloves, and if the purée is thick add some syrup from the cherries; remember that half a cup of wine will be added later.

Cook 10 minutes, add wine, bring to a boil, and serve very hot.

POPPY SEED ROLL
(*Roolet s Makom*)
(sometimes called Mohn Cake)

This is a delicious rich cake made from coffee-cake dough, which is rolled out and covered with a poppy seed and honey mixture, then rolled up, jellyroll style, and baked in a loaf tin.

Plan ahead before making this cake, because the poppy seeds should soak in water overnight before they can be used.

This cake freezes well.

Filling:

½ pound poppy seeds
¼ cup unsalted butter, soft
½ cup buckwheat honey
2 tablespoons heavy cream

1 cup coarsely chopped walnuts
½ cup raisins
1 teaspoon grated orange peel

Soak the poppy seeds overnight in "just-boiled" water—use just enough to cover the seeds. The next morning drain them. Some people insist on grinding the seeds, but it is unnecessary.

Cream the butter and honey together with a wooden spoon.

Add the heavy cream. Then stir in the poppy seeds, nuts, raisins, and orange peel.

The dough:

4 packages dry yeast or 2 ounces compressed yeast
1 cup lukewarm milk
½ cup sugar
1 teaspoon vanilla extract
½ teaspoon grated lemon rind

3 eggs
¼ teaspoon salt
4 to 5 cups flour
½ cup soft, unsalted butter
1 egg mixed with 1 tablespoon milk

Dissolve the yeast in lukewarm milk. Let sit for 5 to 10 minutes until the yeast foams up.

Add the sugar, vanilla, and lemon rind. Beat in the eggs and salt.

Add enough flour to make a medium-soft dough, mixing thoroughly. Work in the soft butter with your hands.

Knead the dough on a floured board for 10 minutes, adding more flour if necessary. When the dough is shiny and elastic and has small blisters on the surface it has been kneaded enough.

Form the dough into a ball and place in a greased bowl; turn dough over to grease on all sides. Dust the top lightly with flour.

Cover the bowl with a towel and place in a draft-free place to rise (30 to 40 minutes), until double in bulk. It has risen enough when it is no longer springy when you poke your finger in the surface.

Punch down the dough with your fist, and knead briefly.

Cut the dough in half. Roll half out on a floured board to make a rectangle less than ¼ inch thick and 9 inches wide. Spread half the poppy seed mixture evenly over the dough. Roll it up jellyroll style.

With butter, grease a 9-by-5-by-3-inch loaf pan. Fit the roll into the pan and let it rise for another ½ hour, or until double in bulk.

While it is rising, preheat oven to 350° F. and prepare the remaining ingredients to make another roll.

Before baking, brush the tops of the rolls with egg mixed with milk. Then bake until golden brown, 20 to 30 minutes.

A NOTE ABOUT THE DOUGH:

It will keep for 3 days in the refrigerator, but it will keep rising. The first 3 to 4 hours it will rise often and must be punched down or the dough will sour. After it is thoroughly chilled it will need to be punched down no more than 3 times a day.

LITTLE POPPY SEED ROLLS *Boolichky c Makam*

These are triangular-shaped rolls, a full four inches on each side, stuffed with poppy seed filling.

In Russia these are sold in almost every snack bar, as we sell miniature coffee cakes and brownies in individual packets.

A basic yeast dough (see Irina's *piroshky dough*) is traditionally used for this. Also, the filling is made without nuts and raisins and grated orange peel, but I think they make a nice addition.

1 *batch Irina's* piroshky *dough (see page 214)*
1 *batch poppy seed filling (see preceding recipe) with or without nuts, raisins, and grated orange peel*

GLAZE: *1 egg and 1 teaspoon milk*

Prepare the dough and filling as directed in their respective recipes.

Roll out the dough to ¼ inch thickness; cut into 4-inch squares.

Put several spoonfuls of filling in the center of each square. The more the merrier.

Take one corner and fold it over to meet the opposite corner, covering the filling and making a triangular shape. Seal the edges well by pinching them together with your fingers. Make an attempt to completely camouflage the seams—the better you do this the less likelihood there will be that leaky little poppy seed rolls will result.

Preheat the oven to 350° F.

Place the rolls on a buttered cookie sheet and let them rise for 20 minutes while the oven warms up.

Brush the tops of the rolls with an egg mixed with a teaspoon of milk. Then bake them for 30 minutes or until they are a rich golden brown.

MENU

*Cauliflower and
Grape Salad
Vegetable Stew
Spicy Chicken
with Meatballs
Chestnut Dessert*

CAULIFLOWER AND GRAPE SALAD
(*Salat eez Tsvyetnoy Kapoosty ee Vinograda*)

This is a peculiar-sounding combination of fruits and vegetables, but the textures and flavors work beautifully together. It is a salad of cooked cauliflower, fresh grapes, and tomato wedges on a bed of lettuce served with sour cream dressing. It is the Caucasian version of health salad Kiev-style. (The Caucasus is the vineyard of Russia, thus the grapes are the distinctly Caucasian aspect of the salad.)

1 *small cauliflower*
Milk and water
1 *small head Romaine lettuce*
1 *large tomato*
½ *pound seedless grapes*

½ *cup sour cream*
¼ *teaspoon lemon juice*
Sugar, salt, pepper to taste
1 *tablespoon chopped dill or parsley (optional)*

Remove the green leaves from the cauliflower and cut the stem flush with the bottom flowers so the cauliflower has an even base to stand on.

Put the cauliflower in a pot that barely contains it and pour in just enough water to cover it. (Measure the water as you pour it in.) For every 4 cups of water used, add 1 cup of milk. (The milk will keep the cauliflower white.)

Boil until tender—not mushy, preferably a little crisp and undercooked.

When (under)cooked, put the cauliflower in a colander and run cold water over it. Let it drain. Then put it in a plastic bag and refrigerate for at least 1 hour.

Assembling the salad:

Wash and dry the lettuce and arrange enough leaves to cover the bottom of a shallow serving dish.

Cut the tomato into small wedges, about eight of them.

Wash and dry the grapes and remove from stalks.

Cut the cauliflower into individual flowerets.

Arrange the tomatoes, grapes, and cauliflower neatly on top of the lettuce bed.

Mix the sour cream, lemon juice, salt, pepper, and sugar together. Then pour over the salad, and sprinkle chopped dill over all.

Chill for at least ½ hour and then serve.

VEGETABLE STEW
(*Tooshoniye Ovoshy*)

Vegetable stews are common in Middle Eastern cooking. They can be eaten hot or cold and are great *zakoosky* or accompaniments to meat. This particular one has zucchini in it, which is my own addition to the recipe. It was originally called Ukrainian vegetable stew, but for the sake of authenticity I've avoided attributing this recipe to any particular area of Russia.

1 onion
Lots of olive oil
½ pound carrots
1 pound tomatoes
2 green peppers
A 1-pound eggplant

1 or 2 zucchini (optional)
1 tablespoon sugar
Salt and pepper to taste
4 tablespoons lemon juice or
the juice of 1 lemon

Dice the onion and lightly brown in some heated olive oil in a large frying pan that has a cover.

Remove the onions from the pan and put them in a large bowl (this bowl will eventually be holding all the browned vegetables).

Dice or slice the carrots (slice if small); they can't be very big hunks or they won't cook. Brown the carrots in a little bit of oil. Then remove from the pan and add to the bowl.

Cut the tomatoes into 1-inch cubes, brown them in oil, and add to the bowl. Dice the green peppers, brown them, and add to the bowl.

Cut the top and bottom off the eggplant, cut it in half the long way, then cut each half in half again the long way. Then cut into 1-inch cubes. Brown in oil and add to the bowl.

Peel the zucchini and cut into 1-inch cubes. Brown and add to the bowl.

Now take all the vegetables, put them back in the frying pan, add the sugar, salt, pepper, and lemon juice and cover the pan. Simmer for about 10 to 15 minutes, or until the carrots are not too hard.

Serve.

SPICY CHICKEN WITH MEATBALLS

Unfortunately, Anna Markievich can't remember the Russian name for this chicken dish. It's made of browned chicken parts coated with paprika and braised with small juicy meatballs in a cream sauce flavored with onions and garlic.

2 3-pound chickens, cut up
Oil or butter
1 pound chopped meat (mixture of pork, beef, and veal)
1 raw egg
2 teaspoons chopped fresh parsley

Salt and pepper
About 1 tablespoon paprika
1 onion, thinly sliced and separated into strings
4 large cloves garlic, chopped fine
1 cup chicken stock
½ cup heavy cream

GARNISH: sprig of parsley

Brown the chicken parts a few at a time in some oil or butter, in a 5-quart casserole. Remove the browned parts and put aside. Reserve the fat in the casserole.

Mix the chopped meat, egg, parsley, and some salt and pepper together. Form into small meatballs—no bigger than 1 inch in diameter. Brown the meatballs in the bottom of the casserole, adding more oil if necessary. Turn off heat.

Now sprinkle the chicken parts with salt and pepper and about 1 tablespoon paprika. Put them into the casserole, arranging it all neatly; distribute the meatballs well.

Add the onions and garlic to the casserole. Pour the chicken stock and cream over everything.

Let the dish simmer, covered, for about 40 minutes, or until the chicken is cooked. (Test by piercing chicken with a fork. If the juice that runs out is white, then the chicken is cooked. If the juice that runs out is red, shudder and let the chicken cook some more.)

Transfer the chicken to a serving dish, arranging the pieces attractively, or unattractively, if you insist. Pour the cream sauce and meatballs over the chicken, garnish with a sprig of parsley and a light sprinkling of paprika.

Serve with some nice, freshly cooked vegetables—carrots and broccoli add color to the table. Also, make sure there's plenty of fresh bread on the table to sop up the sauce.

CHESTNUT DESSERT
(Kashtanovoye Sladkoye)

This dessert is made with chestnut purée and whipped sweet cream. The predominant flavoring is rum or brandy, and there is chopped candied ginger that cuts through the rum if you happen to chew it. It is a pudding dessert that is served in glops on each plate.

This is not a mouth-watering description, so I want to add that this is one of my favorite desserts. Even one of those chronic dieters (my mother) *shamelessly* helped herself to seconds.

Sweetened chestnut purée:

(2 CUPS)

1 pound peeled chestnuts or 1 pound unsweetened unadulterated chestnut purée (comes in cans, sold in gourmet cooking stores)
2 vanilla beans

Approximately 2 cups of milk
⅔ cup sugar
¼ cup water
1 tablespoon soft, unsalted butter

Simmer 1 pound of peeled chestnuts, or the contents of a 1-pound can of unsweetened, unadulterated chestnut purée, in enough milk to cover a vanilla bean that has been slit the long way, with the seeds scraped into the milk. Simmer for 20 minutes.

Discard the vanilla bean. Drain the chestnuts thoroughly and rub them through a sieve.

In a heavy saucepan combine ⅔ cup sugar with ¼ cup water and a 1-inch piece of vanilla bean. Cook the syrup until it forms a soft ball when dropped in cold water. (Start testing it after it has been cooking 5 to 10 minutes.)

Discard the vanilla bean and *immediately* (or else the sugar syrup will harden) combine the syrup with the puréed chestnuts, working the mixture thoroughly until it forms a thick paste. Cool it to lukewarm and stir in the tablespoon of soft butter.

The dessert:

2 *cups sweetened chestnut purée (homemade or a 1-pound can)*
¼ *cup chopped toasted almonds*
¼ *cup rum or brandy*
2 *tablespoons finely chopped preserved ginger*
1 *cup heavy cream, set in the freezer for 15 minutes before whipping it*

Beat the chestnut purée with the almonds and rum (or brandy) and ginger until it is light and fluffy.

Whip the heavy cream until it holds firm peaks when the beater is lifted out of the bowl.

Fold the cream into the chestnut mixture, thoroughly.

Mound the mixture lightly in a serving dish.

Chill well before serving.

MENU

*Cranberry Soup
Peasant Style

Georgian-Style String
Beans or Spinach

Homestyle Beef Stew

Coffee Cream*

CRANBERRY SOUP PEASANT STYLE
(*Broosnika Soop po Derevensky*)

This soup is a refreshing, tart—but not too tart—hot soup. It needs only 1 tablespoon of sugar, and even *that* can be omitted, making this one of the few low-calorie Russian dishes.

1 *cup raw cranberries*	1 *tablespoon sugar*
4 *cups water*	*Pepper to taste*
2 *medium onions, chopped*	½ *cup beet juice and 1 cup*
2 *cups shredded cabbage*	*canned diced beets, or 1*
2 *teaspoons salt*	*cup fresh diced beets*

GARNISH: *sour cream (buy an 8-ounce container)*

Wash the cranberries, and then put them in a pot with the 4 cups of water. Let the cranberries simmer, uncovered, for about 20 minutes, or until soft. Then take a wooden spoon and mush up the cranberries.

Add the raw, chopped onions and shredded cabbage to the pot. Season with the salt, the sugar, and then pepper to taste.

If using fresh beets, add them now. Let simmer, uncovered, for another 20 minutes, or until the beets are just tender enough to be easily pierced by a fork or knife.

The soup can be refrigerated at this point until ready to heat up and serve.

If using canned beets, add them to the pot along with their ½ cup of liquid when you are heating the soup up just before serving.

Serve the cranberry soup piping hot with a dollop of sour cream floating in each bowl.

GEORGIAN-STYLE STRING BEANS
(*Boboviye Stroochky po Groozinsky*)

These string beans with eggs come out almost like a pudding. The string beans are first boiled. Then they are highly seasoned and mixed with eggs. They are cooked in a round pot over a low flame until the eggs are set. They are then unmolded, and the final product is a round-shaped string-bean pudding. It is the vegetable version of a jello mold, substituting eggs for gelatin—if you can imagine it.

2 pounds string beans, washed and trimmed (frozen beans may be used)
3 tablespoons butter
5 eggs

1 tablespoon chopped fresh coriander or parsley
2 tablespoons chopped fresh dill
Salt and pepper
Optional: fresh tarragon, chopped, to taste

Boil the string beans until they are cooked.

Put the beans into a round casserole dish and neatly and compactly toss with 3 tablespoons of butter, which should melt in a minute over the hot beans. Let them cool.

Beat the eggs with the coriander (or parsley), dill, salt, pepper, and tarragon.

Pour the eggs over the beans and cover the casserole dish. Cook for approximately 20 minutes over a low flame, until the eggs are set.

When the eggs are set, run a spatula around the edge of the casserole dish, and then unmold it by turning it upside down over a dish and wiggling it until it falls out.

Serve piping hot. You can make it in advance and just warm it up in the oven before serving.

NOTE:

This vegetable dish needs a lot of seasoning, so don't be too stingy with the salt and pepper!

GEORGIAN-STYLE SPINACH *Shpinat po Groozinsky*

> 2 *pounds spinach, boiled, drained, and chopped*
> 2 *onions, minced and sautéed*
> 5 *eggs, beaten*
> *Salt, pepper and ground nutmeg*
> 2 *teaspoons coriander, chopped fresh*
> 2 *teaspoons chopped fresh dill*

Follow the same method for cooking as with the green beans in the preceding recipe.

HOMESTYLE BEEF STEW, IRINA
(*Ragoo po Domashny*)

When I was in Moscow, Hannah Kaiser asked her maid, Irina Styepanovna, to make a beef stew that is covered with dough and served in individual ceramic pots. This dish was served all over Russia, and she thought it would be a good one for my book. Irina said she had never made it herself, but she did know what it was and thought she could make one.

This is a very old classic peasant dish. The meat requires no browning, nor do the vegetables. It has simple spices—parsley, dill, and salt and pepper—yet it tastes wonderfully seasoned. Hardly any liquid is added to the stew, yet it produces a fantastic broth. The trick is the dough covering used for baking. The dough is a simple flour and water mixture, kneaded well to make it strong and tough. It works on the same principle as a porous, unglazed clay pot cover, except that it has a perfect seal. It manages to lock in all the flavors in the stew as well as cook the meat, potatoes, and carrots in an hour.

In old Russia, the flour used for the dough was very cheap, and the cooked dough was thrown away. But this was not just an act of extravagance. Another reason to throw it away is that it is incredibly tough to chew: it is of granite consistency. Irina forgot to tell us this, and we had a fun time trying to cut the dough, to get at the stew, and even more fun trying to eat it.

This dough has several advantages. It makes the dish look very pretty and delicious. It keeps the meat piping hot until opened, and it gives bored or fidgety guests something to play with at the table. It's a riot trying to peel it off the sides of the dish.

(4 SERVINGS)

3 tablespoons unsalted butter

2 pounds boneless beef cut into
   1-inch cubes

1 large onion, thinly sliced and
   then coarsely chopped

4 medium carrots, peeled and
   cut into thick rounds

1 large potato, peeled and cubed
   (½-inch cubes)

1 tablespoon chopped fresh dill

2 tablespoons chopped fresh
   parsley

Salt and pepper

Dough:

3 to 4 cups flour

1 teaspoon salt

1 cup water

First, decide whether you want to serve this in individual pots or one big pot. Instead of pots, soufflé dishes may be used.

Dot the bottoms of the pot(s) with butter (2 tablespoons in all).

Put in a layer of meat chunks; if you are using only one pot, put in all the meat, and do the same for the vegetables.

Cover with a layer of chopped onions. Cover that with a layer of carrots, and then a layer of potatoes.

The dill and the parsley get sprinkled over all of this. And, finally, season to taste with salt and pepper. (Don't mix anything up, it should get cooked in layers, in this order!)

Dot the top of the stew with the remaining tablespoon of butter, and pour in ¼ cup of water—stock or red wine can be substituted, but it isn't necessary. It tastes fine without any fuss.

Make the dough:

Combine the flour, salt, and water. Add as much flour as you can, to make a good firm, strong dough, kneading it thoroughly for about ten minutes once it is en masse.

Divide the dough into however many parts are necessary for your number of pots.

Roll the dough out on a floured board into a circle.

Cover each pot with a dough circle and press the edges firmly against the sides of the pots. You should feel that you are making a drum.

The stew is ready for baking. It can be refrigerated until 1½ hours before serving.

Bake at 375° F. for 1 hour. Turn off the heat and let it sit in the closed oven for an additional ½ hour.

With a hammer and chisel, open the top of the dough. Then stir up the ingredients, and serve.

COFFEE CREAM
(*Krem Koffyeny*)

This is a kind of coffee ice cream, except that gelatin holds the cream together instead of the freezing. It is flavored with real coffee, so it is far superior to any commercial coffee ice cream. It can be made without the gelatin and just frozen; it is just as good. As a matter of fact, I'm not even sure what the advantage of making it with gelatin is. To make the choice, decide how cold you want the dessert to be and whether you would rather have a type of ice cream or jello.

> 2½ *cups heavy cream*
> ½ *cup freshly ground coffee*
> 6 *egg yolks*
> 1 *cup sugar*
> 1 *packet gelatin*
> ½ *cup warm water*

First put an empty 6-cup mold in the refrigerator.

Bring the cream to a boil. Remove from heat, add coffee, and put aside for 30 minutes. Strain the coffee cream.

Meanwhile, beat the egg yolks with a whisk, gradually adding all the sugar. Continue beating until the yolks are somewhat fluffy and almost white in color.

Dissolve the gelatin in the ½ cup warm water and add to coffee mixture. Mix well.

Pour into the chilled mold and either refrigerate until it sets (4 hours) or serve it frozen.

To unmold, dip the bottom of the mold in hot water, count to 10 slowly, and hold a plate over the mold. Invert the whole business and . . .

Eat.

The Samovar

A SAMOVAR is literally a self-boiler. The big bulbous lower section holds water that is heated by a flame underneath. The hot water can be let out through a faucet on the side of the "tank." On the top of the samovar there is a tiny teapot. Very concentrated tea is stored there. When someone wants some tea, he or she puts a few drops of this very concentrated tea in a cup and then dilutes it with the hot water from the lower portion of the samovar.

"Russian tea" comes from China, packed in little boxes that are wrapped in skins with the fur side inwards to keep the tea flavorful. It is the old-fashioned equivalent of vacuum packing or wrapping things in plastic wrap. You might find Russian tea that has a subtitle of "caravan tea." This is supposed to be fancy because it means it was brought from China by land, not sea. It is said that if the tea is brought by sea, the humidity weakens the flavor.

Tea also comes compressed in a tablet form: *Plitochnyee chai*. It also comes in heavy bricks: *Kirpichnyee chai*. This

The Samovar

kirpichnyee chai is drunk mostly by the Kalmuks and Caucasians. (By the way, they drink it with milk, butter, salt, and pepper.)

Tea is drunk from glasses or porcelain cups. The men all drink from glasses in metal holders—sort of like soda glasses. The women used to have their own unique porcelain cup. Some were handed down from a relative or chosen by the individual. The women *never* used glasses for their tea. I have no idea why.

The tea was either sweetened with honey or jam, or soured with lemon. When jam was used to sweeten the tea, it was served in a little glass saucer. One would put some jam in one's mouth and then have a sip of tea. My Russian grandmother sucks on a sugar cube or a hard candy as she sips her tea.

The tradition of sitting around a samovar in the evening developed from the long cold evenings during the winter, when there was absolutely nothing to do. In Gorky's description of his childhood, he has many descriptions of the evening samovar. There were always some sweets to eat with the tea and one of the men played the balalaika, or someone told stories. Basically it was a long lazy evening.

The samovar itself radiates a lot of heat, so it was natural to gather around it on a cold winter evening. Furthermore, the metal glass-holders get extremely hot from the tea, tending to burn one's hands. In the winter, when there is insufficient heating, this is a very desirable effect. Keep these two points in mind during the energy crisis!

In the Soviet Union today, there are many shops called "Tea Shop," "Russian Tea," or perhaps "The Samovar." I walked into one hoping to buy a nice big samovar and some fancy teas to take home. It turned out to be a tea parlor. There was a huge (but, alas, electric!) samovar standing on a table, and an assortment of French(!) pastries, and *piroshky* filled with meat, or apples, and assorted open sandwiches called *bootyerbrody*. There were two old ladies wearing embroidered peasant blouses, aprons, and embroidered kerchiefs around their heads. They were both overweight, just as they're supposed to be. And they bustled around, making tea for my friend and me, asking and answering questions, suggesting cakes to taste. They were genuine *babushkas*, so called because that's the name for the embroidered kerchiefs they wear around their heads. The word also means "grandma"—and that's what they're all like. They practically adopted me the minute I walked in the store.

If you ever go to the Soviet Union and are feeling depressed or oppressed by the severity of the city you are in—stop in one of these tea shops. If you don't find two warm old ladies to greet you, you can at least sit next to the samovar.

RUSSIAN TEA BREAD
(*Sdobny Hlyebets*)

The recipe for this perfect bread to have with butter and jam and tea came to me indirectly from someone's Siberian grandmother. The lady who was doing the photocopying of the diagrams for this book was exclaiming over the instructions for the stuffed cabbage and chicken Kiev. Then she volunteered a rhapsodic description of a wonderful tea bread that perfumed the atmosphere. It was given to her by a friend's Siberian grandmother. It is her absolute favorite. She said she gave the recipe to many people, but as far as she knew, no one ever bothered. It is quite easy to do, and if you don't have the time to wait for risings, it can safely rise in the refrigerator (covered with plastic wrap) for several hours. It is the sort of goody that can become an after-dinner habit.

(TWO 9″ x 5″ x 3″ OR THREE 8″ x 4″ x 2″ LOAVES)

3 packets dry yeast
¼ cup lukewarm water
1 cup milk
3 eggs, slightly beaten
½ cup sugar

1 teaspoon vanilla
1 teaspoon salt
5 cups flour
¼ pound butter, softened

Dissolve yeast in lukewarm water.

Heat milk to lukewarm.

In large mixing bowl combine the dissolved yeast, milk, eggs, sugar, vanilla and salt.

With large wooden spoon mix in half of the flour, to make a batter. An electric mixer can be used until the dough becomes too heavy.

Beat in the softened butter.

Gradually add the remaining flour until the mixture starts to leave the sides of the bowl clean.

Turn dough onto floured board and knead until dough is smooth and elastic and blisters.

Place in greased bowl and turn dough so that the top is greased too. Cover with a towel and set in warm place to rise until double in bulk (45 minutes to 1 hour). Punch dough down and knead briefly. Let rise a second time in greased covered bowl until doubled in bulk (20 to 30 minutes).

Turn onto floured board and divide into two or three pieces, knead and shape into loaves. Place into buttered loaf pans and let rise.

Preheat oven to 375° F. while the loaves rise. Bake for 25 to 30 minutes until browned and hollow sounding when tapped. Cool on Rack.

Old Russian Holidays

CHRISTMAS
Rojdyestva

T H E following are excerpts from a book called *A Vagabond in the Caucasus* by Stephen Graham:

The Russians are a hospitable nation and, above all things, like to keep an open house. On the great feast days everyone is *at home*—and everyone is also out visiting. That is, the women stay at home and superintend the hospitalities and the men go the rounds. At Moscow it is a full-dress function . . . At Lisitchansk (a small town in Little Russia) it is less polite and more hearty than in the old capital and one makes no distinction of persons.

Graham describes part of the Christmas celebration in this little town:

Before us, on the table, stood the allegorical dish of dry porridge, eaten in memory of the hay and straw that lay in the manger in which the child Jesus was laid. . . . A huge bowl, full of boiled honey and stewed fruit, was set in the middle of the table . . .

. . . The deacon explained its significance to me . . . The Communion is a death feast; Koutia is in memory of His birth. "It is just a special Communion service," said he, "and it is held only once a year." He explained how each dish represented the manger: First we put the porridge in the dish, which was like putting straw in the manger. The mother helped each of us to the porridge; she stood for Mary, who would, of course, see that there was plenty of straw so that it might be soft and warm. Then we each helped ourselves to honey and fruit that symbolised the Babe. We made a place in the porridge and then poured the honey and fruit in. The fruit stood for the body; the honey stood for the spirit or the blood. "Blood means spirit, when one is speaking of Christ," said the deacon . . .

. . . Koutia remained on the table and guests came and partook of the meal . . . the guests would return home by a different way from that by which they came—in order to escape Herod.

The vagabond and his host then take an evening walk:

. . . and presently we saw a group of carol singers carrying what appeared to be a lantern. When we came nearer we found them to be a group of boys carrying a pasteboard star. The centre of the star was clear and a candle was fixed so that the light shone through . . . When we looked closer we found that there was a picture of Christ in the centre, so that the light shone through the face. The chief boy carried the star and the next to him twirled the points. It was an interesting point that they made no collection; though, I am told, they all got a few coppers on the morrow. It was a very charming representation of the Star of Bethlehem. It made its whole journey whilst we were getting home, for we saw it finally enter the church, which, it may be supposed, they considered the most fitting place for the star to rest. . . . We saw stockings outside several cottage doors. It apparently is the custom to hang them outside, so Santa Claus has not to solve the problem of coming down the chimney.

Christmas Eve starts at sunset on December 24 with much praying. The next three days are spent feasting. The "vagabond" describes the festivities:

. . . On Christmas Day alone I ate and drank, for courtesy, at eight different houses. . . . Let me describe the spread. There were, of course, chicken, turkey and vodka, there was suckling, roasted with little slices of lemon. There were joints of venison and of beef, roast goose, wild duck, fried sturgeon and carp, fat and sweet, but full of bones; caviare, tinned herrings, mushrooms, melons, infusion of fruit and Caucasian wines. The steaming samovar was always on the sideboard, and likewise tumblers of tea, sweetened with jam or sharpened by lemon slices. There were huge loaves of home-baked bread, but no cakes or biscuits, and no puddings. At peasants' houses the fare was commoner, but not less abundant, than at the squires. . . .

BUTTER FEAST BEFORE LENT
Maslyaneetsa

One week before Lent is *Maslyaneetsa*. In Old Russia this was a week of carnivals, sleigh riding, and general festivities. The most significant part is the *bliny*: small yeast-risen pancakes, served in huge quantities with butter, sour cream, and vodka. The last day of *Maslyaneetsa* there was a huge afternoon feast. People would come to parties at huge estates. Dressed in formal clothing, the wealthy Russians would sample vodkas and eat obscene quantities of rich *bliny* to counteract part of the vodka's effects. In turn they had more vodka to counteract the richness of the sour cream and butter served with the *bliny*. After at least a dozen *bliny* accompanied by caviar and smoked fish, there was soup, then fish, then salad and some roast meat and perhaps game. Dessert would logically follow. Then there would be coffee, tea, liqueurs, cookies, fruit . . .

At sunset all the festivities would end, and Lent would begin: A seven-week period of fasting. The first four weeks were the strictest—no milk, butter, eggs, cheeses, or fish were to be eaten. People ate only raw vegetables, cold cooked vegetables, and nuts. The fasting gradually became less fierce as the seven weeks passed.

YEAST PANCAKES
(*Bliny*)

The following recipe for *bliny* takes at least five hours to make, accounting for all the rising the batter must do. In Russia they would set half the flour and liquid with the yeast to rise in a crock overnight. This would be somewhat impractical, so the following recipe does not adhere precisely to the authentic traditions.

On Sunday mornings in France, many inns used to serve buckwheat *bliny* for what was called "Khrushchev's breakfast." An American friend of mine had such a breakfast at an *auberge* (inn) near Paris, in the early 1960's. My friend never asked about the ideological background of Khrushchev's breakfast because she thought it was a joke at first ("Why would someone invite an American to a Khrushchev breakfast at a time when Americans were feeling hostile toward him?"), and then—if it wasn't a joke—there was no point in being impolite . . . So she went to the breakfast: they served plates of hot *bliny* topped with sour cream and chopped onions; there were platters of smoked sturgeon, smoked salmon, and pounds of the best caviar. Everyone helped themselves to the fish, putting some of each on top of each pancake.

If you're ever feeling rich, and/or have something worth celebrating, ignore the ideology, or make up some to suit yourself, and bear Khrushchev's breakfast in mind: it would make a glorious brunch.

And if you are wondering why the Russians came up with *bliny* for pre-Lent feasting and the rest of the world did not . . .

Ancient Slavic peoples worshipped the sun, and there was a great spring festival to welcome back the sun after the winter darkness, which took place around the spring equinox. Round, flat cakes, *bliny*, were created in the sun's image and eaten in the sun's honor.

Bliny need not be eaten only before Lent; they are great appetizers, although they have a tendency to get addictive:

> "And what about some pancakes?" his hostess suggested.

For answer, Chichikov rolled three pancakes together, dipped them in melted butter, and dispatched them into his mouth, afterward wiping his hands and lips with a napkin. Having repeated this operation three times . . .

FROM GOGOL, *Dead Souls*

(ABOUT 36 BLINY; SINCE A RUSSIAN WILL EAT 24 AT A SITTING, THIS IS ENOUGH TO FEED 1½ RUSSIANS, PERHAPS MORE PEOPLE OF OTHER NATIONALITIES)

1 *packet dry yeast or 1 ounce compressed yeast*
½ *teaspoon sugar*
½ *cup lukewarm water*
1¼ *cups all-purpose flour*
1¼ *cups buckwheat flour*
½ *teaspoon salt*

2 *cups lukewarm milk*
3 *eggs, separated*
3 *tablespoons butter*
3 *tablespoons sour cream*
    Pinch of salt, drop of lemon juice

If using compressed yeast, cream it with the sugar and then add the warm water.

If using dry yeast, combine the sugar and yeast and water. Let stand for 10 minutes until the yeast has dissolved and starts bubbling.

While the yeast is acting up, measure the 1¼ cups of white flour and ¾ cup of buckwheat flour and the salt into a large mixing bowl.

Pour the lukewarm milk into the flour mixture, then add the yeast mixture. Stir with a wooden spoon, incorporating all the flour, until a nice soupy, smooth batter is made.

Cover the bowl with a towel and let it sit for 2 to 3 hours in a warm place until it is light and bubbly and just about double in bulk.

Beat down the mixture to get the air out of it, and stir in ½ cup more buckwheat flour.

Cover and let rise again for about 2 hours—or until double in bulk.

Meanwhile, separate three eggs.

Fifteen minutes before the batter has finished rising, warm 1 cup of milk and melt 3 tablespoons of butter. Let them cool until lukewarm.

Stir the melted butter, the 3 tablespoons sour cream, and 3 egg yolks into the warm milk. (If the milk is too hot the yolks will curdle.)

When the batter has risen, whip the 3 egg whites in another bowl with a pinch of salt and a drop of lemon juice. Whip them until the whites hold firm peaks when the beater is removed from the bowl.

Fold the egg whites into the batter.

Cover the batter and let it rise for another ½ hour. (This last rising time can be longer than ½ hour—once I made them for an appetizer and after dessert we all had a yen for more *bliny*. As I said before, they tend to be addictive, so I made another batch with the leftover batter that had been sitting out on the counter, covered, for about 2 hours. They tasted fine.)

Heat a griddle or heavy skillet, *lightly* grease it with butter (don't use gobs of butter or the *bliny* will turn a funny gray color although they will still taste good). Without stirring the batter, ladle it out in spoonfuls to make 3-inch rounds.

Flip the *bliny* over when they are perforated with bubbles and the bottoms are lightly browned.

Brown the other side and remove from the pan; start stacking them. Either keep them in a warm oven (250° F.) while you are using up the batter, or have people eat them fresh off the griddle. (This gets tricky when you are trying to entertain.

That's probably why Russians had maids and cooks if they could afford them.)

Serve with a bowl of melted butter and a bowl of sour cream at room temperature. Brush on the butter and spoon on some sour cream and/or put on some caviar or smoked, pickled, or salted fish.

Vodka is as important as the butter and sour cream. The vodka should be drunk first, then followed by *bliny* to counteract the vodka. Then have more vodka to counteract the richness of the *bliny*—and so on until you have a "happy" party!

LENT
Vyeleekee Post

After the *Maslyaneetsa* comes Lent, "the great fast." There are no specific traditional recipes for this time except Dried Mushroom Soup, Vegetable Borscht, and Eggplant Caviar, which are given elsewhere in the book. Anything vegetarian will do.

The following excerpt from Gorky's *My Childhood* shows how one family took Lent very seriously. Most of Russia—especially the poor—felt this way. This strict attitude toward Lent—a seven-week meat and dairy fast—helps explain the excitement of Easter.

One night in Lent I was passing the Rudolfs' house . . . I crossed myself and said: "Christ will rise again and his enemies will be scattered." At this he gave a little squeak and somersaulted down from the roof into the yard. — That got rid of him! The Rudolfs must have been cooking meat and of course he caught wind of it and came to enjoy the smell, so pleased he was that it was Lent and they were eating meat.

The "he" who squeaked in the above passage was of course the devil.

EASTER
Paskha

Easter is the most emotional, exciting, and elaborate Russian religious celebration. People often wonder why Russians pay so much attention to Easter and relatively little to Christmas. Russian Easter is so important because it is really a Christianization of an old Slavic tradition of celebrating the spring. After the long, fierce Russian winters, spring is an awakening in every sense of the word. Stravinsky described spring as being his favorite season in Russia because it came all at once—it was almost as though the earth exploded.

In so many of Dostoevsky's stories, people have their spiritual renewal at Easter time. This may seem trite to Americans, but to Russians the meaning is significant. Winter meant scarcity of food—and, conveniently, the seven-week Lent fast occurred during the slack end of the season. It meant being confined to one's house for several weeks at a time. Therefore, the long barren winter finally blossoming into a big and beautiful spring was paralleled by a long and strict Lenten fast that culminated in a dramatic Easter feast.

Anna Markievich, the Russian woman who gave me the Easter recipes (among others), invited me to attend the Russian Easter service in Syosset, New York. The service itself was four hours long, starting at midnight. There were no seats but I experienced no fatigue or boredom.

The church was made out of a room in an old mansion that was tucked away in the woods just off a main highway. It felt like a different world—completely cut off from America and the city. The parking lot felt sacred, the grass, the trees, the sky, the very air felt holy. There was something intangible in the air that filled my lungs with awe and that made it feel sacrilegious to speak.

The service began at midnight. But a half hour before people had been filling up the little room. People approached Christ's casket, knelt on the floor before it and then prayed, and asked for forgiveness.

The choir was made up of a dozen people—it seemed rather makeshift, and so I was shocked and thrilled by the powerful and beautiful sounds they made. Their chanting had a mesmerizing effect; their songs were magnificent.

Each of us carried a small, burning, white candle that illuminated our faces in the dimly lit room; the church absolutely reeked of incense, and the combination of sight and smell was enchanting.

The service began with the booming sound of a bodiless baritone. For about two hours, the choir sang while the priest performed mysterious duties, some in a little room behind the "stage," and some in front, which included chanting and swinging his incense burner around Christ's coffin. At one point, people started removing all the plants and flowers that surrounded the coffin. The priest symbolically peeked into the casket and discovered that it was empty. Before he made any announcement to the effect that Christ had risen, the congregation began circling the church in search of Christ. This procession symbolizes the disciples' initial hesitation when they discovered that Christ was missing from his coffin.

Before the procession began to move, the candles that lit up the ikons and those on the large candelabras were extinguished. Soon the whole church was dark except for the shining candles that the congregation held. Some men came down the center of the church carrying crosses and banners with pictures of the Madonna and Child on them. They proceeded through the center doors followed by the still-singing choir, the altar boys, and then the priests, holding the candled candelabras, and finally the people.

The procession made three rounds of the church, and as the singing, shining, bodiless faces passed by me, a single bell was tolling rhythmically.

By the time the procession stopped, the church was completely dark, and empty. The singing stopped and the priest, as he swung the incense burner, cried out the long-awaited declaration: "*Khreestos voskresse!*" His call was echoed by the congregation outside. And once again he shouted, and once again the people responded. Finally, with the fullest possible conviction he cried: "*Khreestos voskresse ee vie ee stonoo voskresse!*" ("Christ is risen and truly he is risen!") And the people enthusiastically supported his declaration.

Everyone filed back into the church, which was once more light. We had left it in darkness, symbolizing Christ's death, and we reentered in light to symbolize his rebirth.

The service continued as before, with chanting and singing. At one point in the middle of the service, many of the women left the chapel with one of the priests. They went onto the back porch of the mansion, where there was a large picnic table laden with beautiful baskets covered with embroidered cloths. Each woman had brought a basket of the traditional Easter foods to be blessed by the priest. The women would take the blessed baskets home after the service so that their families would have some "holy" food with which to break the fast.

The priest lifted up the embroidered cloth of each basket,

sprinkled holy water and said a blessing. Each basket was more beautiful than the one before—the women all competed with one another to make the fanciest and biggest basket. Inside each basket was a *kulich*, a rich, sweet yeast bread, in the shape of a tall cylinder with a frosted mushroom-shaped cap. *Paskha*, a sweetened cheese, butter, and egg mixture, in the shape of a pyramid, was standing beside the *kulich*. There was often a piece of Russian sausage, *kolbasa*, a dish of salt, and a small loaf of communion bread.* And of course there were the beautiful Russian Easter eggs called *pisanky*, which are supposed to protect the people from disasters. (The more *pisanky* made each year, it is said, the better the year will be.)

After all these foods had been blessed, the women and the priest returned to the chapel to participate in the rest of the service. The traditional liturgy follows the special Easter section of the service, and that in turn is followed by communion. The people line up to be spoonfed the wafer and wine from a golden spoon by one priest while another priest wipes their chins and mouths with a cloth.

Then the congregation lines up again, and the priest hands each person a brightly colored hard-boiled egg and says, "*Khreestos voskresse*," and they kiss each other three times: once on the right cheek, once on the left, and once on the lips (the last kiss has been modified, in our inhibited times, to another kiss on the right cheek). Then there is a confusing flurry of *Khreestos voskresse*s and kisses and after a while it doesn't seem to matter who is greeting whom.

And then there is the Easter feast . . .

First you eat the hard-boiled eggs. They symbolize longevity and endurance in honor of the fact that you have just survived another Russian winter and Lenten fast.

*For an explanation of the communion bread and salt, see page 155.

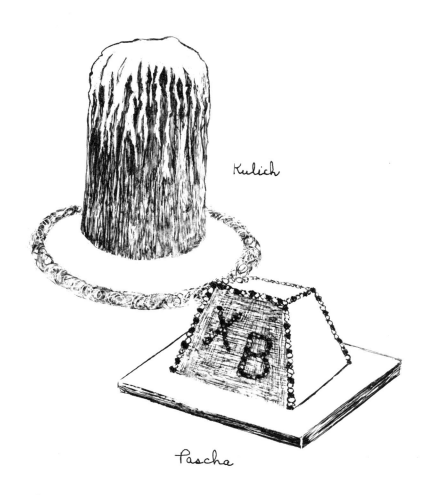

Kulich

Pascha

Second, you take a slice of *kulich* and a piece of *paskha* and eat them. The *kulich* represents the cakes and breads you have been abstaining from during the fast. It is a very rich and heavy bread cake. The Russians use such a rich bread because they haven't had any for such a long time; it's sort of a "super-bread." The *paskha* is made from pot cheese, a large-curd, dry version of cottage cheese, butter, egg yolks, sugar, and candied fruits. It is very smooth and sweet and rich, and almost addic-

tive. This dish symbolizes the dairy foods that were not al-
lowed during Lent—and like the *kulich* it is a super conglom-
erate of all the foods it is representing.

Next you have a piece of *kolbasa*. The reason you have to save
the *kolbasa* for last is that you have abstained from meat
longer than any other food and it would be too much to break
the fast with it immediately. *Kolbasa* is usually made with different types of meat, and it is very spicy—and so it is the repre-
sentative of all the kinds of meat that you haven't been able to
eat for such a long time.

If all this rich food seems rather excessive to you, remember
that in Russia, meat, fish, milk, butter, and eggs were either
difficult or impossible to obtain during the last months of winter. Then at the time of Russian Easter (a week or two later
than the European and American Easter), spring would have
arrived, the rivers thawed—fresh fish available and transportation for fresh meat, vegetables, and dairy products possible. . . .

Easter certainly occurs at a logical time for a feast celebrating a rebirth—whether it be Christ's or the earth's.

ANNA MARKIEVICH'S KULICH

NOTES ON KULICH:

1. All ingredients should be room temperature before
starting.

2. Melt and clarify the butter *first*, so that it has time to
cool. (Clarify means skimming off the scum after the butter
has melted; keep only the clear liquid.)

3. This recipe halves very nicely.

4. The dough takes about 4 hours to rise the first time. The
second rising is a little more than 1 hour. At first I thought I

might be doing something wrong, but then I read a description of a preparation for Easter in a Russian home and it told of the cooks setting the *kulich* to rise overnight in the kitchen. If you want it to rise quicker, double the amount of yeast: it won't affect the flavor.

While the *kulich* is rising, may I suggest going to a movie, reading a good book, or cooking something else.

(10 TO 15 SERVINGS)

4 *packages dry yeast or 2 ounces compressed yeast*	14 *egg yolks*
1 *cup lukewarm milk*	½ *cup honey*
8 *cups white flour*	⅓ *cup light rum*
3 *cups sugar*	2 *teaspoons vanilla extract*
1 *cup melted and clarified butter (at room temperature)*	10 *egg whites*
	2 *teaspoons salt*
	Citron, candied peel, nuts, yellow raisins, to taste

Mix the yeast, lukewarm milk, 1 cup of flour, and a tablespoon of sugar. Let stand, and while the yeast is activating . . .

Stir the butter, and the 1½ cups of sugar until the sugar is dissolved.

Beat the egg yolks into the butter and sugar two at a time.

When the yeast, milk, and flour mixture is double in bulk and foaming, add it to the butter and yolks. Beat.

Mix the honey and rum together and add to the butter and yolks. Keep beating. Then gradually add the rest of the flour, the egg whites, and salt, and keep beating.

The dough is a thick batter. If you have an electric mixer with a kneading hook, knead with it. If you only have your hands: Put one hand in the goo and knead it in the bowl. This is not conventional kneading—concentrate on folding lots of air into the batter.

Cover the bowl with plastic wrap, and then with a thick terrycloth towel. Put in a very warm draftfree place (an unlit gas oven is terrific: it keeps the dough nice and warm), and surround it with pillows or towels to protect it against any shock: it's very delicate and might sink if someone slams a door. Let rise for 3 or 4 hours until double in bulk. Meanwhile find something creative to do with yourself.

Beat down the risen dough. Butter 3 or 4 2-pound-size coffee cans. Put a round piece of parchment paper in the bottom of each. Fill each can with batter to the halfway mark.

Let the dough rise again, covered as before in a warm place, but not in the oven, since you have to preheat it.

After the *kulich* has been rising for ½ hour to 45 minutes, set the oven at 350° F.

When the *kulich* is ready, bake for 30 minutes to 45 minutes—until the tops are golden brown and when a skewer stuck inside comes out dry and clean. If the tops brown too quickly, moisten a paper towel and cover the browned cap. This feeds moisture into the *kulich*, besides keeping the cap from burning.

When the *kulich* is done, remove from oven and let cool for 15 minutes (a full 15) in the cans.

Meanwhile, take a pillow and cover it with a soft towel.

Wiggle the *kulich* out onto the pillow. If it doesn't budge, run a knife along the inside edge to separate it from the can; but be careful that the knife is right next to the edge or you will mutilate the *kulich*. If the *kulich* is still stubborn, *wait* a few more minutes. When it is ready it will come out. Don't be impatient! Learn from *my* mistakes!

The pillow will protect the *kulich* from any bruising that it would get if left to cool on a rack. It also dries the outside and leaves the inside of the bread very moist. It also makes the pillow smell very nice.

Icing:

Stand the cooled *kulich* up. Pour the following frosting on top of the *kulich*, so that it covers the "cap" and drips somewhat down the sides. Or, to quote Anna: "On your little hills of mushroomed *kulichy*—pour the white icing."

> ½ cup heavy cream
> 2 teaspoons almond extract
> 1½ cups confectioner's sugar

Mix the cream with the extract; then, stirring constantly with a wooden spoon, gradually add the sugar until the mixture is smooth and creamy. (This is a thin icing.)

To serve:

When the frosting has dried, slice off the cap of the *kulich*, and cut round slices from the column-shaped bread. In Russia, a huge *kulich* would stand on the table for a week, a slice would be cut off as I've instructed, and then the cap replaced to keep the raw surface from drying out.

Serve with a piece of *paskha*.

ANNA MARKIEVICH'S PASKHA

NOTES ON PASKHA:

1. Uncooked *paskha* will last 1 week in the refrigerator.

2. There are a few options: adding rosewater is desirable if you can find it. Try fancy French and Middle Eastern food stores. Almonds, finely ground, can also be added, but they make the *paskha* gritty, and as my friend Anna Markievich says: "The *paskha* must be smooth, so I don't add the almonds because I don't like to hit grit." Citron and candied fruit rind may also be chopped up and added. Anna's response to this is: "My family is too lazy to chew the citron and rind, besides

they don't like it. I just add the maraschino cherries, one of those small jars."

3. The vanilla bean rather than extract is important.

4. Buy good-quality pot cheese. The delicatessen section of the supermarket or a good cheese store should carry the large-curd, nongritty, smooth pot cheese. The best pot cheese can be bought in one of the Jewish cheese stores in downtown Manhattan, such as Miller's on Essex Street.

5. It is also important to let the *paskha* drain for 1 or 2 hours unrefrigerated. Once it is cold it drains slowly, and the most liquid will come out in that first hour. Don't let it drain *all day unrefrigerated*; it will get rotten and taste funny, and later you will feel funny.

6. The list of ingredients calls for 18 hardboiled egg yolks. If you don't have any use for 18 hardboiled egg whites, I suggest first separating the raw eggs and then poaching the yolks in gently simmering water for about 10 minutes. Be careful not to overcook the yolks or they will be rubbery.

(12 TO 15 SERVINGS)

1 *vanilla bean*
1 *pint heavy cream*
½ *pound unsalted butter (at room temperature)*
1 *pound sugar (more or less, according to your taste)*
5 *pounds large-curd pot cheese*

18 *hard-boiled egg yolks*
2 *teaspoons rosewater (optional)*
1 *small jar maraschino cherries and/or citron and candied rinds (optional)*
Ground almonds (optional)

DECORATION: *maraschino cherries or mixed glazed fruits*

Slit the vanilla bean and scrape the seeds into the heavy cream. Put the bean into the cream as well, and let soak in the refrigerator while you prepare the cheese.

Cream the butter and sugar together. When the sugar is dissolved, slowly add the pot cheese and keep creaming it.

Mash the hard-boiled egg yolks and gradually add them to the cheese mixture.

Either put the cheese mixture through a food mill or mash it through a sieve or cream it in a mixer. Put it through the mill or sieve 3 *times*, or blend the cheese in a mixer until it is perfectly smooth.

Remove the vanilla bean from the cream. Then with a rubber spatula, fold the cream into the cheese mixture.

At this point you have a lot of options: add the rosewater, maraschino cherries, almonds, citron and candied peel.

Line a large flowerpot with cheesecloth. Carefully put the *paskha* into the pot. Fold the ends of the cloth over the top of the cheese and place a plate on top that is a little bit smaller than the top of the flowerpot. Put a weight (cans of food, bricks) on the plate and set the pot on a cake rack over a plate. Let the *paskha* drain for 1 hour unrefrigerated.

Refrigerate and let drain for at least *two days*.

To serve:

Unmold by inverting the flowerpot over a plate. Peel off the cheesecloth. (Sometimes the unmolding doesn't work too well, and it's usually because the *paskha* is still too wet. The *paskha* will taste wonderful but will look deformed. To make it look normal, just reshape it on the serving plate with a spatula.)

Decorate the *paskha* with maraschino cherries or mixed glazed fruits. It is traditional to have the initials *xb*, signifying "Christ is risen," on the side; they used to be automatically imprinted by the old wooden *paskha* molds, but you can create them with the chopped fruits.

Serve it with a slice of *kulich*.

NATASHA'S BOILED PASKHA

Boiled *paskha* is just as good as raw *paskha,* and it lasts longer. This was important in Old Russia, because the *paskha* was often left out on the table for the whole day next to the *kulich.* The *kulich* was kept moist by replacing its mushroom cap after each slice, but raw *paskha* had a tendency to turn sour. Boiled *paskha* lasts much longer.

Anna Markievich got this recipe for me from her friend Natasha. Natasha is an elderly woman who speaks hardly any English, even though she emigrated before the Russian Revolution. I consider this recipe a real prize, first of all because it's very good, but secondly because boiled *paskha* making has become a lost art with the advent of the refrigerator.

1 *vanilla bean*	1 *pound sugar*
½ *pint heavy cream*	*Chopped maraschino cherries or mixed fruits (optional)*
5 *pounds nongritty pot cheese, large-curd*	
1½ *pounds unsalted butter (at room temperature)*	1 *cup ground almonds (optional)*
10 *raw egg yolks (at room temperature)*	

DECORATION: *maraschino cherries or mixed glazed fruits*

Take 1 tall vanilla bean and slit it lengthwise. Scrape out the seeds into the cup of heavy cream. Put the scraped bean into the cream also. Let soak while you play with the rest of the ingredients.

Sieve the pot cheese or put through a food mill. Do this 3 times or more, until it is absolutely creamy.

Cream the butter with a wooden spoon, then add to the cheese. Beat the yolks and add to the cheese. Mix the cheese, yolks, and butter until fully combined.

Transfer the cheese mixture to a pot. Put it over a low flame and, stirring constantly, bring it to a simmer. (This is similar to making a pudding.) When the mass begins to liquefy, remove the vanilla bean from the heavy cream and add the cream to the cheese mixture.

Now, still stirring constantly, add the sugar gradually. *Do not let it boil.* Keep it simmering until the sugar is completely dissolved.

When the sugar is completely dissolved, bring the mixture to the boiling point by raising the heat slightly. Remove from the flame immediately and stir in almonds and fruit if you intend to put them in at all.

Let the *paskha* cool.

Line a giant clay flowerpot with cheesecloth and then transfer the cooled cheese to the flowerpot.

Set the flowerpot on a cooling rack set over a plate. Refrigerate 2 to 3 hours before applying weight. Any liquid that accumulates on top should be poured off. When the mixture has solidified somewhat, put a saucer on top of the cheese and lean down on it with all your weight, thus squeezing a lot of liquid out of the *paskha.*

After this initial press, lay some bricks or heavy cans or weights on top of the saucer and let the *paskha* drip, unrefrigerated, for about 1 hour. Then refrigerate the *paskha,* still weighted down, for at least 2 days.

Unmold the *paskha* onto a plate, reshape it if necessary, and decorate with maraschino cherries or glazed fruits, making the initials *xb* somewhere on the side.

Serve with a slice of *kulich.*

NOTE:

Don't worry if, when you are unmolding the *paskha*, you discover the cheesecloth is sadly twisted in *and* around the cheese. You can push the whole thing back together with a spatula and nobody will know the difference.

ANNA MARKIEVICH'S KOLBASA

Kolbasa is a very pungent sausage. It is full of garlic and spices. Anna Markievich, who gave me the recipe, never uses measuring cups or spoons. She would figure out how much garlic and other spices to put in by smelling. As we gradually added the chopped garlic, she would bend over the bowl, take a deep breath . . . and then a big smile would light up her face; she would shake her head from side to side, close her eyes, and with a blissful expression on her face say, "Almost . . . just a little bit more!" Then I would add another ½ teaspoon, she would smell it, and, finally, her head rocking back and forth, she would smile—it was almost as though she had received a message from God: "It's just right. I can feel it through my nose."

This *kolbasa* is the best sausage I have ever tasted. Mrs. Markievich gave my family some to take home Easter evening, and all of us couldn't get over how fantastic that sausage tasted. That particular piece of sausage had been blessed, but the *kolbasa* tastes terrific even when it isn't.

The cabbage recipe that follows the *kolbasa* recipe is traditionally served with the *kolbasa*. Both of these can be used as *zakoosky*.

This is another one of Anna Markievich's superb recipes. She spent an entire afternoon making the *kolbasa* with my mother and me. Her original recipe calls for 50 pounds of meat, but she reduced it to 5 pounds for the sake of this book.

This sausage can be made with all pork butt, which Anna Markievich prefers, or veal, beef, and pork can be used. The Estonians would use three different types of meat. No offense to the Estonians but I would take Mrs. Markievich's word and make the *kolbasa* with all pork.

The meat must be ground on the coarse grind: this is sometimes called the sausage grind. If not, you will have to add more seasoning, because the finer grind absorbs more of the flavoring.

Then comes the problem of casings. Casings are a euphemism for intestines. I thought it would be disgusting and that I would never be able to handle it. But it's no more disgusting than handling the meat or muscle of an animal or cooking lobes of calves' liver for dinner.

Casings can be bought cleaned and ready for use at a butcher store. They are more expensive than salted intestines, and the cleaning process is fun and easy. One pound of casing should be enough for fifty pounds of sausage. (The salted casing will last for a year in the refrigerator.)

(12 TO 15 SERVINGS)

5 *pounds pork butt, ground on the coarse blade or "sausage grind"*

3 *cups water*

4 *teaspoons (about 8 cloves) minced garlic (Mince it with ½ teaspoon salt.)*

2 *tablespoons soy sauce*

4 *teaspoons freshly ground black pepper*

1 *teaspoon cracked mustard seeds*

2 *teaspoons caraway seeds*

2 *teaspoons fennel seeds*

3 *tablespoons coarse salt*

2 *tablespoons chopped fresh dill (1 tablespoon dried)*

2 *tablespoons chopped fresh parsley (1 tablespoon dried)*

½ *pound sheep or hog intestines*

Mix the meat with the water. It should be nice and slippery and soft. You may need to add more water if you didn't get the sausage grind, but simply ordinary grind.

Peel and then smash the garlic with a knife and mince it with ½ teaspoon of salt. The salt makes it easier to chop it fine. Put the minced garlic in a bowl.

Add to the garlic the soy sauce, ground pepper, cracked mustard seed, caraway seeds, fennel seeds, coarse salt, dill, and parsley.

DIGRESSION:

Points on the spices:

1. The soy sauce gives the meat a nice color and adds salt.

2. Fennel seeds keep the *kolbasa* from "repeating." That means you won't burp up the *kolbasa* and keep tasting it for a few weeks.

3. This is Anna Markievich's system for grinding the pepper and smashing the mustard seeds: Take the peppercorns and put them in a towel. Place on a hard surface and smash with a hammer until pulverized. For the mustard seeds: Place in the towel and hammer until they are cracked—not pulverized.

Preparing the casings:

Soak the casings overnight in fresh, cool water. Then, when you are ready to use them, unravel one casing—that is, untangle it. Find the end of it and fumble around looking for the hole. Stick your finger in the tube and put it (the tube) under the faucet, running cold water through it. You will only need about 4 inches of water—then let the water flow through the casing.

The casing is not as delicate as it looks. It is very strong! Be bold. Remember that it held up under a lot more pressure during the animal's life!

It is now ready for stuffing.

Stuffing the casings or making the sausage:

Stretch the casing over the end of the sausage stuffer as one would slip on a stocking (the stuffer being the leg). When stretching on the casing, hold the end you are feeding to the stuffer somewhat taut and keep the circumference of the tube round by pushing the part of casing that is lagging behind up onto the stuffer.

When the whole casing is on the stuffer, leave an inch of casing hanging. Tie a knot at the end of the casing.

Now put the meat, a little at a time—actually, you won't have much choice: put in as much as your grinder can cope with—into the grinder.

Start grinding. It may take a little while for the meat to start coming out. The sausage should be about 1 inch to 1½ inches wide. Gradually pull more casing off the stuffer as you need it. Do this slowly or the sausage will be too thin. If an air pocket develops, push the sausage back onto the stuffer, and wait for more meat to fill in the pocket, then gradually slide it back off, waiting for it to get filled.

Important: If you discover a hole in the casing, stop grinding and cut the casing at the tear. Squeeze some meat out of the end of the interrupted sausage, and make a knot in the extra casing now hanging down. Then pull some casing off the stuffer. Cut it. Tie a knot at that end of the shortened sausage. Start all over again with the remaining casing that is on the stuffer. Don't let the sausage ever be shorter than 4 inches.

Repeat this process until you are out of meat or casing—or both.

Cooking the sausage:

If you have a nice butcher, ask him to hang the sausage for 2 days so that it will season. If not, don't worry about it.

Put the *kolbasa* in a pot that is just about 3 inches too tall for it. Cover with hot water, and bring to a boil. Then cover the pot and simmer for 20 to 30 minutes.

Test the sausage at this point: Put a crochet hook (a needle may be used, but this is the authentic butcher's method) in the side and if the juice that comes out is cloudy, it needs more cooking. If the juice is clear, pour the water into a bowl and *save* it for cooking the traditional cabbage accompaniment. Put the sausage in a colander to drain.

Now either freeze or refrigerate it until you want to serve it.

Just before serving: Broil the sausage until it is browned, then turn it over and broil the other side. Serve with the cabbage. (That's in the next recipe—don't miss it; it's terrific.)

CABBAGE FOR KOLBASA
(*Kapoosta*)

(12 TO 15 SERVINGS)

The sausage-boiling liquid (see above)	1 bay leaf
	½ teaspoon peppercorns
8- ounce can tomato sauce	2 onions, sliced
4 pounds sauerkraut, rinsed and drained	½ teaspoon caraway seeds
	A little flour to thicken

Reduce the liquid reserved from the sausage to half the original quantity by boiling it rapidly, uncovered.

Add to it the tomato sauce, sauerkraut, bay leaf, peppercorns, sliced onions, and caraway seeds.

Cook, covered, for 1 to 1½ hours. At the end of the cooking, cook uncovered for a little while to get rid of some of the liquid.

Then add a little flour mixed with some water, and simmer to thicken.

Serve hot with the *kolbasa*.

VARIATION ON KAPOOSTA

(6 SERVINGS)

3 *tablespoons butter*
1½ *pounds drained and rinsed sauerkraut, or shredded fresh cabbage*
¾ *pound apples, peeled, cored, thinly sliced*
1 *carrot, peeled and shredded*
2 *teaspoons sugar*
Salt and pepper

Melt the butter in a 2- or 3-quart saucepan and add all the other ingredients.

Cover the pot and simmer for 15 to 20 minutes until the cabbage is soft; if the cabbage looks dry at any point, add a little bit of water.

Serve hot.

NOTE:

You can add some dried fruits and assorted nuts—it makes a good vegetarian lunch.

OLD RUSSIAN WEDDINGS
Svadbee

Russian wedding traditions evolved from the pagan practice of having the bridegroom kidnap the bride to the groom paying for the bride to the Christian practice of blessing the marriage in the church. Blessings of engagements and marriages were taken seriously only by the nobility. The common people either did not know about this rule or ignored it and until the 1400's the only recognition necessary for the marriage was that of the community.

Russian Orthodox weddings were once the product of parental decisions: The couple to be married often did not know each other and never had any say in the matter. (This has changed and now the parents do not make the choice, although it is still customary to ask their blessing.) The young man would come to the girl's house to present her parents with his marriage proposal. If the parents approved, a servant would enter the room carrying a tray full of champagne-filled glasses. The servant would then drop the tray on the floor for good luck. The two young people would kneel before an ikon to receive the blessing of both sets of parents.

The marriage ceremony is announced in church a few weeks before the marriage. Communion for the engaged couple takes place the Sunday before the wedding. Similar to Western practice, the bride and groom are separated for twenty-four hours before the wedding and the groom is not supposed to see his bride's gown.

The wedding service, I have been informed, is very moving and mystical, as is the Easter service I described earlier. Russian religious songs are beautiful and the chanting is mesmerizing.

First the bride enters the church, with her veil covering her face. The priest and groom greet her at the entrance and the engagement is reconfirmed.

With the bride standing on the left, the groom on the right, the priest joins their hands and says a special prayer. The bride's veil is pulled back and the couple proceeds down the aisle to the center of the church. The main part of the service now begins.

Groomsmen have to hold heavy crowns over the heads of the couple, but since the service is so long, the groomsmen all take turns.

The priest gives the bride and the groom each a lighted candle, which they hold during the service. Rings are exchanged three times. The couple sips the sacramental wine and then, the priest leading them, the couple proceeds around the congregation three times. All the "threes" are references to the Holy Trinity.

The parents of both the bride and groom are not present at the service. They are waiting wherever the reception is, probably panicking about the food and the other details of a party. When the married couple comes to the reception, they are welcomed into the house by both sets of parents with the traditional bread and salt. Bread and salt are symbols of prosperity. They are considered to be the absolute essentials; as long as there is bread and salt in the house, there is nothing to worry about. They are also symbols of respect and loyalty. Bread and salt is not only served at weddings but is also presented to guests as a sign of welcome.

The wedding feast or breakfast is huge. (Sounds like all the other Russian feasts, doesn't it?) There is champagne and loads of food—meat and vegetables, bread, cake . . . During the feast, the guests shout out, "*Gorko, Gorko!*" ("Bitter, bitter!"), in response to which the bride and groom kiss to sweeten the meal. Long ago, the very rich, of course, had an orchestra playing throughout the meal, all formal and fancy. But whether the families were extremely wealthy or not, special wedding candy was served. These were little bars of chocolate or some other candy wrapped up tightly in satin, which was sewed or glued together and trimmed with lace. A little decoration was fixed on top of these little packages, perhaps a tiny bouquet of orange blossoms, or a figurine. (This same type of candy was served at court balls, with tiny framed pictures of the royal family attached on top.)

WEDDINGS IN THE SOVIET UNION

The contemporary wedding ceremony has become a very simple and efficient affair. I watched a wedding in Kharkov, a city in the Ukraine. Nobody seemed to mind that a group of forty American tourists walked in to watch the wedding.

The wedding ceremony is actually a registration and nothing more. If you are religious, you can then go and have a church or synagogue wedding, but that is no longer common.

In the Soviet Union, one can marry at the age of eighteen.

Couples first have to apply for a registration date. The earliest point that they can marry after that is two months. This waiting period is to give the couple time to think the matter over.

The Palace of Togetherness, or The Wedding Palace, was made from an old mansion. In a fancy, mirrored waiting room, three or four couples in full wedding dress sit chatting with the six or seven people who are going to attend the ceremony. Of this six or seven people, two are the witnesses.

The bride's witness must be a woman, and the groom's must be a man. It is a symbol of good luck to have unmarried witnesses.

The actual registration takes about fifteen minutes. The Deputy of Soviets presides and makes a well-wishing preamble. Then there is some recorded wedding march music while the bride and groom approach the dais where the Deputy and his/her assistant are sitting. They sign in, and leave the dais.

Then the witnesses sign, and leave the dais, returning to a spot twenty feet from the Deputy's table.

The assistant to the Deputy then brings the rings on a small silver dish, and the Deputy brings the certificate down to the couple. The couple is congratulated, and the rings are placed on the fourth finger of the right hand.

The friends of the couple say, "Gorko!" and the couple kiss to get rid of any bitterness.

And then the next couple comes in.

There are some remnants from the old church weddings. For example, the parents never come to the service because they are preparing for the party afterward. And "Gorko, Gorko!" is said, just as it was in Old Russia. The difference is that the State weddings lack pageantry, glamour and warmth. One finds it hard to cry or feel excited when the couple only looks mildly content about the whole affair. A spectator can feel no joy on hearing a feeble murmur of "Gorko," and watching the couple kiss perfunctorily.

The State service certainly doesn't waste any time, but I would hate to have my wedding like that. It may be embarrassing to have your mother crying at your wedding, but it's also part of the fun.

I followed one of the wedding groups after the ceremony. The couple and their attendants went in decorated taxi cabs over to a statue of Lenin and left a bouquet of flowers. I saw other couples leaving their flowers on a monument to the men killed in World War II.

That was one of the depressing things about my visit to the Soviet Union. I had been hoping to see the world Tolstoy had described. I had forgotten that a lot has changed since the era of St. Petersburg society.

COMMUNION BREAD
(*Prosfeera*)

Communion bread is used at weddings as a traditional sign of welcome and also as the communion bread in the church service. (At Easter communion, the bread has the initials *xb* on top in pieces of dough—standing for the Old Slavonic words *Khreestos voskreese,* meaning "Christ is Risen."

The name *prosfeera* comes from the word *prosfornee. Prosfornee* are the widows of the lesser clergy, and these women made little rolls that were used for communion—*prosfeera.* (These can be made by pouring the batter for the large communion bread into buttered muffin tins—filling them half full.) Loads of these little rolls were brought to the priest at an ordinary mass. The priest would symbolically divide the batch of rolls into five parts. The first part was for Christ; the second for Mary; the third for the Apostles, prophets, and martyrs; the fourth for the living, and the last for the dead.

The recipe I have provided for the *prosfeera* is a batter bread. This means it requires no kneading, so it is very little trouble to make. It is a rich yeasty, eggy, buttery dough that produces a light-textured, self-glazing, beautiful bread.

(10 TO 12 SERVINGS)

¼ *pound unsalted butter (at room temperature)*
4 large eggs (at room temperature)
1 ounce compressed yeast or 2 packages dry yeast

3 tablespoons sugar
1 cup lukewarm milk
4½ cups flour
1 teaspoon salt

Cream the butter. When it is soft, add the eggs one at a time and beat until they are completely mixed into the creamy butter.

Dissolve the yeast with the sugar and lukewarm milk.

Add 2 cups of the flour and the salt to the butter and eggs and mix completely. Add the yeast mixture and beat. Add the rest of the flour and beat.

When the dough, or thick batter, is completely mixed and smooth, cover the bowl with plastic wrap and then with a thick terrycloth towel and set in a warm place to rise. I put it in an unlit oven. The rising will take about 1 hour. When the dough is double in bulk, beat it down with a wooden spoon.

Grease a 10-inch-diameter, 4-inch-deep spring-form pan. Pour in the batter, and let it rise for ½ hour to 1 hour, until double in bulk, or until it just reaches the top of the pan.

Meanwhile, preheat the oven to 375° F.

When the bread has risen, bake for ½ hour. It is self-glazing, so don't brush it with egg. It comes out a beautiful, glossy, and golden brown.

Remove from the spring-form pan, and from the bottom, after it has cooled for 10 minutes.

VINAIGRETTE SALAD WITH BEETS
(*Vinegret eez Syvokly*)

Vinaigrette salad, made with beets, is a salad of boiled vegetables. It is traditionally served as the first appetizer at Russian Orthodox weddings.

In the winter, no fresh cucumbers are used in the salad—only pickles. No matter what season it is, however, some pickled cucumbers are used because of their flavor.

I watched the Intourist Restaurant (Moscow) chef, Boris

Lavroff, make this salad. The salad will taste good no matter how shloompily you put it together, but it can be made to look rather dramatic. Lavroff has a way of curling cucumbers, cutting tomatoes so they look like roses, and arranging them all so they don't look ridiculous. If you have a creative eye for design, you can make this into a great-looking appetizer. If you have a destructive eye for design, don't worry about it; all the food gets mixed up inside us anyway.

(4 TO 6 SERVINGS)

½ pound beets, boiled, peeled, sliced thin, and then cut into ½-inch squares
8 new potatoes, boiled and sliced, then cut into ½-inch squares
3 small pickles (half-sour cucumbers), cut into cubes
1 small cucumber, cut into cubes
  Green peas, boiled (optional)
½ medium-sized onion, sliced thin and separated into strings

Dressing:

3 parts vinegar and/or lemon juice to 1 part oil
Salt and pepper to taste

Garnish:

Parsley
Sliced onion rings
Long, curled cucumber slices
Tomato wedges
Canned cherries

NAME DAYS
Dyen Rojdyeniya

In Old Russia, everyone was given the name of one of the saints in the Church calendar. That saint's day was the name day of anyone with that saint's name. The saint's day had the same importance as birthdays do today, and it was celebrated by a big party.

Tolstoy describes Natasha's name day celebration in the beginning of *War and Peace*. You will find excerpts from the description of that dinner in the introduction to the chapter on dinners. The following excerpt describes the name day reception before the dinner.

It was St. Natalia's day and the name day of two of the Rostovs—the mother and the youngest daughter—both named Nataly. Ever since the morning, carriages with six horses had been coming and going continually, bringing visitors to the Countess Rostova's big house on the Povarskaya, so well known to all Moscow. The countess herself and her handsome eldest daughter were in the drawing-room with the visitors who came to congratulate, and who constantly succeeded one another in relays. . . .

After receiving her visitors the countess was so tired that she gave orders to admit no more, but the porter was told to be sure to invite to dinner all who came "to congratulate."

The traditional name-day cake is called *krendel*. It is made with a rich yeast dough similar to a coffee cake dough, and it has loads of raisins and candied fruits in it. It is baked in the shape of a pretzel, and then sprinkled with confectioner's sugar and almonds.

RUSSIAN BIRTHDAY CAKE
(*Krendel*)

NOTES ON KRENDEL:

1. *Krendel* should be flavored with saffron, but I have substituted almond and vanilla extracts since saffron is so rare and expensive.

2. *Krendel* can be shaped the way I suggest in the recipe or it can be made into a five-strand braid (each strand having thick middles and tapering toward the ends), and then shaped into a large B.

3. You can add more or less fruits to the dough according to your taste.

(10 TO 12 SERVINGS)

2 *packages dry yeast*
½ *cup plus 1 teaspoon sugar*
½ *cup lukewarm water*
5¼ *cups flour*
½ *teaspoon vanilla extract*
½ *teaspoon almond extract*
1 *cup lukewarm milk*
1½ *teaspoons salt*
1 *tablespoon grated lemon peel*

2 *eggs, slightly beaten*
¼ *pound unsalted butter, softened at room temperature*
1 *cup mixed, chopped glazed fruits and/or golden and dark raisins*
Some melted butter (about half a stick)

GLAZE: 1 *beaten egg*
Granulated sugar

GARNISH: *Toasted almonds*
Confectioner's sugar

Combine the yeast, 1 teaspoon sugar, lukewarm water, and ¼ cup flour. Set in a warm draft-free place to rise and become spongy.

Combine the vanilla and almond extracts, lukewarm milk, salt, ½ cup sugar, and lemon peel. When the yeast mixture has doubled in bulk, add it to the milk mixture.

Put the 5 cups of flour in a large mixing bowl. Gradually beat in the yeast–milk mixture. Then add the 2 eggs. Then add the softened butter—it should be *very* soft; otherwise it will be difficult to incorporate into the dough. Add more flour if necessary to make the dough form a ball and not be completely stuck to the sides of the bowl.

Flour a board and knead the dough for 15 minutes, or until the dough is satiny smooth and free of lumps. Then flatten the dough and work in the glazed fruits and raisins gradually.

Form the dough into a ball and place in a buttered bowl. Cover the bowl with a towel and set in a warm draft-free place (like an unlit oven) to rise until double in bulk (about 1 to 1½ hours).

Punch down the dough, turn out of the bowl, and form into a long "rope" with a fat middle and tapering ends. Form into a pretzel shape.

Place the shaped dough on a buttered baking sheet. Brush with melted butter and let rise again for about 45 minutes. Preheat the oven to 375° F. When the *krendel* has risen a second time, brush with beaten egg, sprinkle with granulated sugar, and sliced, slivered, or ground almonds. Bake for 40 minutes.

Cool on a rack. Dust the top with confectioner's sugar. Serve, eat—and enjoy.

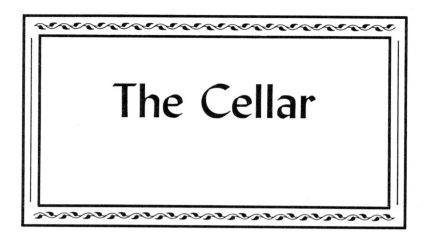

The Cellar

THE winter storage cellar played an important role in Old Russian cuisine. Its modern parallel is the supermarket freezer section, where we can find frozen berries, vegetables, fruit juices, etc., when those fruits or vegetables are not in season. Fruits and vegetables are not often in season in most of Russia. The growing period is less than sixty days in northern Siberia, and less than one hundred days in the northern half of European Russia. Southern Russia, the Caucasus, has a growing period of four to six months, but it is of little help to Siberians in the winter because of insufficient transportation.

During the summer, fruits and vegetables are quickly pickled or dried, or made into jellies or jams. These fruits do not have to be especially sweet and ripe because sugar is added in the marinating process. Dried fruits need no added sugar because the natural sugar has less to sweeten as the fruit shrivels up.

Preserved fruits and vegetables are put in the huge underground cellar in barrels or jars; the dried produce hangs on strings. These cellar foods are not touched until winter, when fresh produce is not available; thus they are an important supply of vitamins. Also, a sudden snowstorm might trap a family indoors for weeks at a time, and, because of the snow, transportation to and from the Caucasus is difficult.

The survival instinct that prompted the development of a cellar cuisine influenced other aspects of Russian cooking. For example, many recipes readily use leftovers, and have that peculiar quality of improving with age. (See *piroshky* [page 214], *shchee* [page 22], *borscht* [page 30], apple *sharlotka* [page 40], and *pelmeny* [pages 225 to 230].)

The following is an excerpt from a very old Russian cookbook. The information may seem useless to you now, but who knows, one day we might run out of electricity and other power, and all our modern science and technology will be useless. You never know when this kind of old-fashioned know-how will come in handy.

STORES, JAMS, SALT PROVISIONS, PICKLES, ETC.*

STORING VEGETABLES

Keep potatoes in a dry cellar in bins. Before putting them in fumigate cellar. Put some sulphur on the ledges, light it, shut the cellar for one night and the next day. Then, the sulphur having burnt out, air cellar thoroughly. Sulphur fumes destroy potato mildew.

Onions should be kept in a dry storeroom, for if kept in a damp place they will give out shoots too early.

Cauliflower and brussels sprouts are stuck, root down, into dry sand, and kept in a dry storeroom.

Cardoons and celery are uprooted and placed in the

---

* From the Borzoi Cook Book, Alfred A. Knopf, 1923

cellar, in sand, without cutting off either leaves or roots.

Carrots, beetroots, celery roots, leeks, are buried in well dried sand.

Cabbages, white and red, are tied in pairs and slung across a pole.

HOW TO KEEP FRESH APPLES

This is the best way to keep a large quantity of apples, pears, etc. Wrap each fruit separately in paper. Prepare a clean barrel, quite dry and odorless. Put a layer of straw at the bottom, then a row of the wrapped fruit, again a layer of straw, again a row of the fruit, and so on. Finish with a layer of straw and shut barrel tightly. Keep in icehouse, if possible on the ice, but be careful that the barrel does not stand in water. Choose winter varieties for storing. Fruit stored in autumn will keep fresh and firm until Christmas.

MARINATED FRUITS
(Marinovanniye Frookty)

Marinated fruits kept in properly sealed jars can be kept in the cellar for the winter fruit supply. The fruits can be almost any kind except perhaps melons. Grapes, cherries, plums, apricots, peaches, apples, pears, etc., can be used. The marinated fruit is nice served as an accompaniment to roast meats or as a dessert with whipped cream or sour cream, or even cottage cheese. I think they even taste good by themselves.

FRUIT MARINADE

6 *cups water*
½ *teaspoon cloves*
½ *teaspoon peppercorns*
1 *tablespoon tarragon or bay leaves*

3 *cups sugar*
1 *stick cinnamon*
3 *tablespoons wine vinegar*

Boil the above ingredients together for 5 minutes. Chill. Pour over properly prepared fruit in jars.

PREPARATIONS FOR MARINATING

APPLES AND PEARS

Wash fruit, put in pot of water. Bring to a boil. Let simmer for 3 minutes. Cut in half, remove core, and stem.

PLUMS, APRICOTS, AND PEACHES

Boil like the apples and pears, but remove the skin.

CHERRIES AND GRAPES

Cook with the marinade as though part of the marinade. Chill, put into jars.

NOTE:

Since I don't know much about sealing marinated fruit jars, I simply refrigerate the fruit in old jars I've saved from commercial jams and it seems to keep for a very long time.

BEETS

Use only 1 cup of sugar in the marinade. Boil or bake unpeeled fresh beets until tender (not mushy!). Slip off the skins and put them in jars with chilled marinade.

IRINA'S SALTED MUSHROOMS
(*Solyoniye Griby*)

Salted mushrooms are an important part of the winter storage foods. They have a lot of important vitamins and keep very well.

In his autobiography *Speak, Memory,* Vladimir Nabokov describes his mother's favorite pastime of picking mushrooms:

One of her greatest pleasures in summer was the very Russian sport of *hodit' po gribï* (looking for mushrooms). Fried in butter and thickened with sour cream, her delicious finds appeared regularly on the dinner table.* Not that the gustatory moment mattered much. Her main delight was in the quest. . . .

Rainy weather would bring out these beautiful plants in profusion under the firs, birches and aspens in our park, especially in its older part, east of the carriage road that divided the park in two. Its shady recesses would then harbor that special boletic reek which makes a Russian's nostrils dilate—a dark, dank, satisfying blend of damp moss, rich earth, rotting leaves. But one had to poke and peer for a goodish while among the wet underwood before something really nice, such as a family of bonneted baby

* A recipe for mushrooms with sour cream appears on page 69.

edulis or the marbled variety of *scaber*, could be discovered and carefully teased out of the soil.

Mushroom picking in Russia is still an important pastime. The variety of mushrooms is enormous—most of them are not available in America. In the Pioneer camps—coed Boy Scout camps—where most Soviet children spend their summers, a point is made to teach the kids how to distinguish poisonous from nonpoisonous mushrooms.

When I was in Kiev, we visited a Pioneer camp. I tried desperately to convince two little boys to show me where to pick mushroom soup. You see, I had a problem—I didn't know the word for mushroom—only for the soup. After they had finished giggling and figured out what the dumb American tourist wanted, they took me mushroom picking. All we could find were two mangy, rotten-looking mushrooms. Apparently mushroom territory was a hefty hike from where we were, and there was not enough time to go down there.

Irina gave me the following recipe for salted mushrooms. The first step may seem a little irrelevant to you, but Irina thought it was very important.

(4 SERVINGS)

1 *pound mushrooms*	1 *bay leaf*
6 *cups water*	5 *cloves*
1 *tablespoon salt*	10 *peppercorns*
2 *tablespoons vinegar*	

First, pick the mushrooms.

Wash them thoroughly.

Put them into a pot with 4 cups of water and the tablespoon of salt. Simmer very gently over low heat, uncovered, for 2 hours.

Meanwhile, prepare the marinade: Mix 2 cups of water, the vinegar, bay leaf, cloves, and peppercorns. Boil for 10 minutes. Remove from heat and cover the pot of marinade. Let it cool.

When the mushrooms have cooked, put them and 1½ cups of the cooking water into a bowl. Add the marinade to the bowl of mushrooms. Mix them around.

For a good balance, put the mushrooms, without the marinade, into jars, filling them ¾ full. Then pour the marinade over them, filling up the jar. Cover the jars and refrigerate until needed. Or if you know how to seal the jars properly, just store them in the pantry.

LIGHTLY SALTED CUCUMBERS
(*Malosolniye Ogurtsy*)

You can tell from the look of the cucumber when it's ready for pickling. As soon as they lose their earthy smell and get their natural smell back, take them and salt them.

GORKY, *My Childhood*

(This was one of the little pieces of wisdom that Gorky remembers his grandmother telling him when he was very young and would follow her around as she did her chores.)

The following are mild pickles. They must be kept refrigerated and will last about 2 weeks. These pickles are similar to the half-sour pickles you can buy in Jewish delicatessens. Lightly salted cucumbers are very good as a side dish with meat or sandwiches.

(6 SERVINGS)

8 *oak leaves—or similar leaves*   2 *peppercorns*
   (They keep the cucum- 10 *whole coriander seeds*
   bers from getting   1 *clove garlic*
   soggy.)   2 *tablespoons salt*
4 *cups water*   1½ *pounds small cucumbers*
3 *sprigs dill*   *(special pickling variety)*

Line the bottom of a jar, or crock, with half the oak leaves.
Add the water and spices—the garlic remains whole.
Add the cucumbers.

Cover the cucumbers with the remaining oak leaves. Then cover the top of the jar or crock. You may need a weight—a saucer with a heavy can on top—to keep the cucumbers from floating to the top. They must be submerged.

Refrigerate for at least 2 days before eating.

ORANGE OR LEMON PRESERVES

This is a marmalade—excellent and easy. A Ms. McGrath sent me the recipe. Russians serve it with toast or in a small glass saucer with tea.

NOTE:

This must stand overnight.

> *Orange Preserves: 4 oranges and 1 lemon*
> *Lemon Preserves: 1 orange and 4 lemons*

Peel the orange(s) and lemon(s) with a potato peeler so that you don't get much pulp. Chop the rind into paper-thin julienne strips.

Remove the pulp (the white stuff outside the fruit and under the skin). Chop the fruit and remove the pits.

Combine the fruit and rind.

Add 1 cup of water for each cup of fruit and peel.

Let stand, covered, for at least 4 hours—preferably overnight.

After the peel and fruit has stood, boil the mixture for 10 to 20 minutes, or until the peel is tender. Cool.

Add 1 cup of sugar for each cup of fruit and juice.

Simmer until the jelly is thick, 20 to 30 minutes. Then pour into hot jars and cool and seal.

If you don't know how to properly seal a jar, just refrigerate the marmalade, or put it in jars that commercial jam comes in.

DRIED MUSHROOMS
(*Sooshoniye Griby*)

Mushrooms—fresh and firm
String

Wash and dry the mushrooms. Skin them.

Make a hole in the center of each mushroom, thread it onto a string.

Dry the string of mushrooms in a slow oven (200 to 250° F.), or out in the sun, on a large cookie sheet, for several hours or days until they are shriveled and totally dry.

Store covered in a dry place.

CARROT AND SAUERKRAUT SALAD
(*Salat eez Morkovy ee Kisloy Kapoosty*)

Carrot and sauerkraut salad is a quickie but goodie. This is actually an imitation of a Russian "preserved" salad, where grated carrots, shredded fresh cabbage, and seasoning are bottled in olive oil. It was therefore served mostly during the winter, when fresh salads were not obtainable. This is, however, an excellent imitation of the original version.

> 2 *cups sauerkraut (1 pound)*
> 1½ *cups peeled and shredded carrots (about 4 carrots)*
> 2 *tablespoons olive oil*
> *Salt, pepper, sugar to taste*

Drain the sauerkraut thoroughly, but do not rinse.
Combine with the rest of the ingredients and put in a bowl or a dish.
Serve like coleslaw.

BREAD BEER
(*Kvass*)

Kvass is a nonalcoholic bread beer. It is made from leftover bread crumbs and stored in barrels kept in the cellar. In the Soviet Union, it is sold on the streets out of big tanks. A lady sits next to her tank and washes glasses as she serves people the *kvass*. One learns to forget hygiene as the lady hands you a grubby-looking glass filled with ice-cold *kvass*. It has a slightly sweet mint taste, and the natural carbonation from the yeast. I love the stuff.

Kvass is used not only as a beverage. It forms the base of an excellent soup, *okroshka* [page 72], and it is used for cooking *boujenina* [page 67], a braised fresh ham.

The following is Gorky's grandmother's advice on *kvass* making:

If you want good kvass, then you must insult it, make it angry. Kvass can't stand sweet things so throw in a few raisins, or some sugar—a small teaspoon to a bucket will do . . .

GORKY, My Childhood

1 pound black bread, dark rye, or pumpernickel (For heaven's sake, don't make the bread; buy an old junky loaf!)
16 cups water
2 packets dry yeast or 1 ounce compressed yeast

¼ cup lukewarm water
1½ cups sugar
2 tablespoons fresh mint leaves or 1 tablespoon dried mint
2 tablespoons raisins

Equipment:

A sieve and a piece of cheesecloth
Bottles—about 3 of the 1-quart size

Bake the bread at 200° F. until it is dried out; slice it first to speed up the process. Then chop it coarsely and put it into a huge bowl or pot.

Bring the 16 cups of water to a boil (that's 4 quarts), and pour it over the bread. Mash it around with a spoon to make sure that all the bread is getting soaked.

Cover loosely with a towel and leave in a warm, draft-free place for at least 8 hours.

When the 8 hours are up, take out another large bowl or some type of vessel. Set a sieve over it. First pan the liquid, if any, off the top of the bread. Then start spooning the wet bread into the sieve, squish it thoroughly with the back of a spoon so that all the juice—or a lot of juice—drips through. Do only a little bit of bread pulp at a time, so you get as much juice as possible. The squeezed-out bread will still be wet and mushy. Don't worry about it, there's a limit to how long you can squeeze the stuff: just throw it away.

When you have extracted all the bread juice you can, sprinkle the yeast over ¼ cup lukewarm water, add ½ teaspoon of the sugar, mix, and then set in a warm, draft-free spot to foam and froth for 10 minutes.

When the yeast has doubled in bulk, mix the yeast into the bread juice. Add the chopped or crumbled mint. Cover the pot or bowl with a towel, and set in a warm, draft-free place for at least 8 hours.

When your 8 hours or so are up, line a sieve with a piece of cheesecloth. Strain the bread juice again, into a big bowl or pot. Using a funnel, pour the strained juice into bottles, filling each one two-thirds full. Divide the raisins amongst the bottles, and drop them in, to get the *kvass* good and angry.

Cover with a piece of plastic wrap or a towel, and let sit in a cool place, but not a refrigerator. A wine cellar will do, or the basement of a house. It should sit for 3 to 5 days, until the raisins have floated to the top of the bottle, and the sediment has sunk to the bottom.

Pour the clear golden liquid into other clean bottles, taking care to leave the sediment behind. (The raisins don't have to be left behind—it's up to you, although I've never found a raisin in a glass of *kvass*.)

Keep the *kvass* refrigerated for at least 2 days, until all the sediment has sunk to the bottom.

To serve: Pour the cold *kvass* through a cheesecloth-lined strainer into a pitcher.

Too Russian to Be Ignored

THIS chapter is dedicated to all those famous Russian dishes that have been severely mutilated by Americans and other well-meaning gourmands. These dishes were too common to include in the menus yet too Russian to be ignored.

CHICKEN KIEV
(*Kooritsa po Kievsky*)

This is the all-time classic Russian masterpiece. It is a boned breast of chicken wrapped around butter, breaded, and deep fried. The most delightful moment is the startling squirt of butter that assaults you when you pierce this harmless-looking little package of meat!

There is an easier preparation of chicken Kiev, but it is not as good. It is made with chopped white chicken meat. This chopped meat is wrapped around a piece of butter, breaded, and deep fried. Using chopped meat eliminates the problem of boning a breast. I mention it because, in the Soviet Union, eight times out of ten you will be served this "lazy chicken Kiev."

The real thing is really very easy to prepare. The fried chicken can be frozen and reheated ½ hour before you are ready to serve it.

It has a few variations; for instance, different-flavored butters may be used—lemon, herb, plain . . . and some people add mushrooms.

Chicken Kiev is traditionally served with boiled green peas in pastry tart shells and shoe string potatoes. I suggest buying the tart shells and the potato sticks—neither are worth the time and trouble to make. (I really should be shot for that last statement. Let me alter it: the tart shells and shoe string potatoes *are* worth making—but, in general, it's not very practical.)

Butters for Chicken Kiev

Melt the butter, clarify it, then let cool to room temperature and mix in the herbs or flavoring. Refrigerate until solid. (Before completely solid, stir the butter in case some of the herbs have sunk to the bottom.)

Herb Butter:

1 cup (8 ounces) unsalted butter
2 tablespoons chopped fresh dill or 1 tablespoon dried
1 tablespoon chopped fresh tarragon or 1½ teaspoons dried
1 tablespoon chopped fresh parsley or 1½ teaspoons dried
1 clove garlic, minced very fine
  Salt and pepper to taste

Lemon Butter:

> 1 *cup unsalted butter with lemon juice to taste*

Shallot Butter:

> 1 *cup unsalted butter*
> 3 *tablespoons shallots, finely minced*
> 3 *tablespoons chopped fresh parsley*
> 3 *tablespoons lemon juice*
>   *Salt and pepper to taste*

The chicken:

> 6 *boned chicken breasts (½ to ¾ pound each), all excess fat, cartilage, skin removed (these are actually half the breast)*
> 12 *tablespoons butter (1½ sticks), chilled*
>   *Salt and pepper*

> ½ *cup flour*
> 4 *egg yolks and 2 tablespoons vegetable oil, mixed in a shallow bowl*
> 1 *cup fine bread crumbs, toasted*
> 1½ *quarts oil or 3 pounds vegetable shortening*

Take each breast and perform the following operations:

Remove the tendon from the breast by grabbing the exposed tip of the tendon with your thumb and index finger. (It helps to wrap your fingertips with paper towel so that the tendon doesn't slip out of your grip.) Then place the back edge of a knife at the spot where the tendon goes under the muscle, the point of unexposure. Press the knife slightly downward and away towards the rest of the unexposed tendon while pulling out the tendon with your papered thumb and index finger.

Separate the breast and fillet and place them side by side on a sheet of wax paper. Place another sheet of paper on top of the chicken.

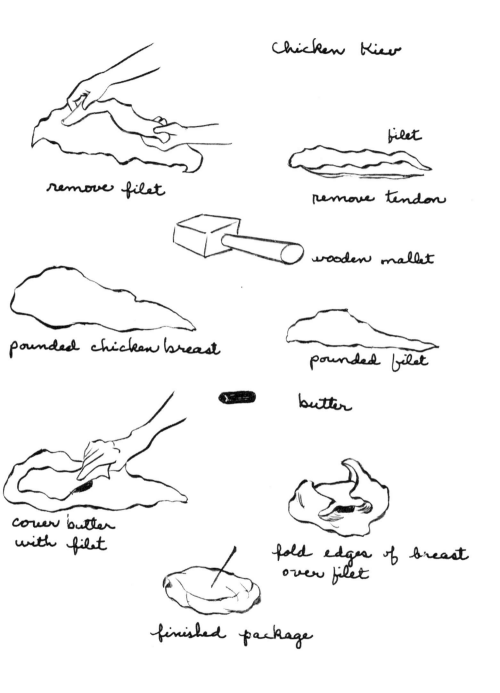

Chicken Kiev

remove filet

filet

remove tendon

wooden mallet

pounded chicken breast

pounded filet

butter

cover butter
with filet

fold edges of breast
over filet

finished package

Pound the chicken with the smooth side of a meat mallet, taking care not to tear the meat. If the wax paper tears, take a new sheet. If the meat does tear, overlap torn edges and pound them together. Flatten each breast to a thickness of an ⅛ of an inch. Don't get it *too* thin!

Place 1 to 2 tablespoons of butter in the middle of the breast and cover it snugly with the fillet. If you are using unsalted butter, salt and pepper the inside surface of one breast before putting in the butter.

Then fold the sides of the breast over the lump of butter; flatten the lump if necessary—but as little as possible.

Fold the ends up and secure the wider end over the narrower flap with a toothpick.

Refrigerate breast while you prepare the others so the butter does not melt.

Remove toothpicks.

Dip folded-up breast in flour, coating the surface. Pat, squeeze it into a triangular shape.

Dip it then in the egg yolk–oil mixture.

Roll it in bread crumbs.

Fry breasts in the fat at 370° F. until golden brown, turning them so they brown evenly on all sides. Do no more than three at a time. This will take about 5 minutes for each batch.

Drain on a plate covered with a double layer of paper towel.

Then, depending on the time, *either* freeze the chicken and reheat in a 350° F. oven for 35 minutes before serving, *or* put in a 250° F. oven for no more than 10 minutes—just to keep them warm.

Serve immediately on a hot platter surrounded by fresh watercress.

BEEF STROGANOFF
(*Bef Stroganoff*)

The story goes that Count Sergei Grigorievich Stroganoff's cook was preparing dinner out in the northern part of Siberia. To his dismay, the sirloin that he had been planning to use for dinner was frozen solid. The only way he could cut the meat was to shave it in very thin slices. So he took the thin slices of beef, sautéed them with some chopped onions or scallions, added some sour cream to make a sauce . . . that's what beef Strognoff really is. The mushrooms and tomato paste are not authentic ingredients for true beef Stroganoff.

In Russia, beef Stroganoff is made either with or without mushrooms. The tomato paste is less common—except in southern Russia, where it is said to have originated.

Russians make this in a double boiler—perhaps Count Stroganoff's cook was using an open fire and placed his pan over a hanging pot of boiling water. The double boiler is not essential, but if you have one, use it.

This recipe should feed 4 to 6 people. It tastes fine the next day, so don't worry about making too much.

The sauce is simple, yet spectacular. Have plenty of bread or rice to sop up the sauce. Because the sauce tastes so good, the meat becomes rather incidental; so, perhaps, if you are on a tight budget use a not-so-expensive cut of meat.

The meat must have all fat and gristle removed, especially the gristle; otherwise it's a challenge to chew.

(6 SERVINGS)

The sauce:

6 tablespoons butter
2 tablespoons flour
1 teaspoon tomato paste
    (optional)
1 cup hot beef stock
½ pound mushrooms
    (optional)

3 tablespoons scallions, finely
    chopped
½ teaspoon garlic, finely
    chopped
½ teaspoon lemon juice
1 to 2 tablespoons Dijon-style
    mustard
1 or 2 tablespoons chopped
    fresh dill (optional)

In a saucepan, melt 3 tablespoons of butter; do not let it brown.

Remove pan from heat; add 2 tablespoons flour. Return pan to heat. Stirring constantly, brown the flour lightly; it should be a creamy beige color. (This is called a "roux.") Add 1 teaspoon of tomato paste if you want to.

Pour in the hot beef stock all at once and stir vigorously to incorporate the roux.

Bring the mixture to a boil slowly over moderate heat, stirring constantly with a wire whisk to keep the sauce smooth. It will thicken after about 5 minutes. Let the sauce simmer gently over a tiny flame.

Meanwhile, if you want them, slice the ½ pound of mushrooms into thin slices.

Melt 3 tablespoons of butter in a frying pan. When the foam subsides, add the chopped scallions and garlic, and sauté until the scallions are limp and translucent; don't wait for them to burn or brown.

If using them, add the sliced mushrooms now; sprinkle with ½ teaspoon of lemon juice. Raise the heat, cook quickly, constantly stirring, until mushrooms are barely cooked through —3 to 4 minutes.

With a rubber spatula, scrape the entire contents of pan into the sauce—i.e., the roux–stock mixture.

Mix 1 to 2 tablespoons Dijon-style mustard into the sauce.

Optional: Add 1 or 2 tablespoons of fresh dill to the sauce.

Simmer the sauce for 5 minutes. Then put aside until 15 minutes before serving the whole dish.

The meat:

> 2 *pounds sirloin steak*
> *Salt and pepper*
> *Some flour*
> 3 *tablespoons butter*

Cut the sirloin into slices ½ inch thick, ¼ inch wide, and 2 inches long. It is easier to do if meat has been slightly frozen, i.e., it is hard.

Remove all fat and gristle.

Salt and pepper each slice of meat and let the meat stand for at least an hour. (It can be left out for 3 hours.)

Shake the slices of meat in some flour in a paper bag, so that all sides are coated lightly.

Melt 3 tablespoons butter in a hot frying pan. Then put in the strips of meat—as many as will fit in a single layer in the pan. Brown the meat on all sides—don't thoroughly cook it. Put it aside until needed.

Assembling the Stroganoff:

> ½ *cup sour cream*
> *Salt to taste*
> *Boiled rice or boiled potatoes as an accompaniment (You might want to serve some bread to sop up the sauce.)*

Russians use a double boiler for this process, but I don't see the necessity. If you have one, use it; if you don't, don't worry; it's no tragedy.

Reheat the sauce. Stir it with a whisk to make it smooth. Bring to a boil gently over the tiniest flame.

Add the strips of beef and turn them over in the hot sauce, coating them completely and heating them through. (You are not cooking the beef; because of the thinness of each piece, they will be adequately cooked from braising and this "reheating" combined.)

With a wooden spoon, a chopstick, or any other utensil, stir in, gradually, the ½ cup of sour cream.

If the sauce is too thick for your taste, add a little more sour cream (or stock). Add salt to taste.

Serve with rice or potatoes—*not* noodles. You need something to absorb the sauce. (Make sure there's some good homemade white bread on the table.)

IRINA'S BEEF STROGANOFF

This is certainly the simplest beef Stroganoff I have ever made—and quite likely the best.

(6 SERVINGS)

1 big onion or 2 small ones	1 tablespoon flour
Butter	Salt and pepper
2 pounds boneless sirloin steak, cut into small strips ½ inch thick, 1 inch wide, 2 inches long	½ cup dry red wine
	1 cup (8 ounces) sour cream
	½ pound mushrooms

GARNISH: *chopped fresh parsley*

Peel the onion, cut it in half the long way, and slice paper thin. Separate the semicircle rings.

Sauté in butter in a large frying pan that has a cover and that is large enough to hold all the meat. When the onions are limp and translucent, but not browned, add the cut-up beef and cook, stirring occasionally, so that the beef browns lightly on all sides. Discard the onions.

Add the flour, salt, and pepper and stir, making sure that the meat gets coated with the flour and seasoning.

Add the red wine, and let it simmer for about 5 minutes. Then stir in the sour cream, and remove from heat. Cover the pan and let it sit while you prepare the mushrooms.

Wash the mushrooms very well. Then put them in a large pot—at least large enough to hold them with 4 inches of pot empty.

Add a tablespoon of salt and enough water to reach an inch below the top of the pot. Bring the pot to a boil. Let boil, uncovered, for 2 to 3 minutes.

The mushrooms are now poached. Drain them in a colander, and then slice them thinly, or if they are mangy looking, chop them.

Add the mushrooms to the beef and stir carefully, distributing the mushrooms as evenly as possible throughout the pan.

Set the entire dish aside until about 15 to 20 minutes before serving. At that time, warm up the Stroganoff in the covered pan, letting it simmer ever so gently over a very low flame.

Serve when it is piping hot over a bed of rice or with potatoes, sprinkled with parsley.

VEAL AND CHICKEN PATTIES
(*Kotlety Pojarskiye*)

Russian *kotlety* are the ancestors of American hamburgers. Any kind of chopped meat, including fowl and fish, is combined with bread crumbs and cream, and fried in butter to create a superlative hamburger.

It is said that sailors from Hamburg, Germany, had eaten chopped beef in Russia, and having enjoyed it so much, they brought the custom back to Hamburg. In the early 1900's, *kotlety* were brought to America by the Germans. Americans gave the credit to the Germans for creating this dish and called the *kotlety* "hamburgers."

Kotlety, made with the meat of young hazel hens (a European woodland grouse) or young partridges and supplemented by a small amount of chopped beef, were served by an innkeeper named Pojarsky in the town of Torzhok, a small town located between Moscow and Leningrad (or what was then St. Petersburg). Torzhok means marketplace in Russian, which suggests that Torzhok was once a commercial center. Many people traveling between Moscow and St. Petersburg stopped at Pojarsky's Inn. Torzhok has since declined in importance. It is now acknowledged for its embroidery and its flax industry and for Pojarsky *kotlety*.

Since hazels hens are hard if not impossible to come by, chicken is a legitimate substitute. Chicken and veal, in a proportion of 3 to 1 are the modern ingredients.

Don't forget to make the sauce! It's very quick and easy and seems to make all the difference. By the way, sautéed sliced mushrooms make a nice addition to the sauce.

(6 SERVINGS)

1 4-pound chicken or 3 pounds
    cut-up chicken
1 pound ground veal
2 cups bread crumbs, from
    fresh bread
1 cup milk
    Salt and pepper

Seasoned flour (¼ cup flour,
    ¼ teaspoon each salt and
    pepper)
Butter for frying (be gener-
    ous)
1 tablespoon vodka
1 cup sweet or sour cream

Skin, bone, and remove tendons and cartilage from the chicken meat.

Put the veal and chicken through the fine blade of a meat grinder twice.

Soak the bread crumbs in 1 cup of milk and then squeeze dry.

Combine the bread crumbs and meat thoroughly with your hands. Season the mixture with salt and pepper, then divide it into six or eight parts and form patties.

Coat each patty with seasoned flour.

Heat a large frying pan and melt the butter. Over medium heat fry the *kotlety* on both sides—about 3 minutes for each side or until they are golden brown.

Remove the *kotlety* from the pan and make the following sauce: Put vodka in the pan juices and add a cup of sweet cream or sour cream, stirring constantly.

Pour this sauce over the meat, and serve.

SHASHLYK AND BASTURMA

Shashlyk and *basturma* are the Soviet versions of *shish ke-bab*: cubes of meat broiled on skewers. These Soviet *kebabs* originated in the Caucasus, where they were cooked on swords over an open fire, and served with pilaf.

Shashlyk is made with cubes of lamb meat marinated in lemon juice and onions. The marinade may seem too simple to experienced *shish kebab* eaters, but trust me—it is enough to tenderize the meat and give it a delicate lemon flavor.

Basturma is made with cubes of sirloin steak marinated in red wine vinegar and onions. Originally it was marinated in pomegranate juice—specialty shops may carry it—but red wine vinegar is the conventional substitute.

SKEWERED LAMB
(*Shashlyk*)

(4 SERVINGS)

Marinade:

> 1 *onion, sliced*
> *Juice of 2 large, juicy lemons*
> 2 *tablespoons olive oil*
> 2 *tablespoons corn oil*
> 1 *tablespoon salt*
> ½ *teaspoon black pepper, freshly ground*

Meat and onions:

> 2 *pounds boneless leg or shoulder of lamb*
> 2 *medium onions*

Mix the marinade ingredients together and pour into a bowl large enough to accommodate the meat.

Cut the meat into cubes: 2 inches by 1 inch by 1 inch. Cut each onion into quarters.

Put the meat into the marinade, toss it around, and make sure it gets coated with the juice and onions. Then put the onion quarters in the bowl; let them get coated too.

Marinate, unrefrigerated, for at least 3 hours. If it feels more sanitary, cover the bowl of meat—but it is not necessary.

Take 4 skewers—metal or wooden. First put an onion quarter on the bottom, then thread on one fourth of the meat cubes. End with an onion quarter. Do this to all 4 skewers.

Heat up a broiler to its highest heat, or have a barbecue similarly set up.

Broil 4 inches away from the flames for 5 to 7 minutes on each side—or until browned nicely.

Serve 1 skewer to each person with a wedge of fresh lemon, *tkemaly* sauce (see below), scallions, and fresh tomatoes.

TANGY PRUNE SAUCE
(*Tkemali Sos*)

(ENOUGH FOR 2 BATCHES SHASHLYK)

1½ teaspoons chopped fresh basil or ¾ teaspoon crumbled dried basil

2 teaspoons chopped fresh coriander leaves (cilantro)

1 teaspoon imported cayenne pepper

¾ teaspoon salt

¾ teaspoon chopped garlic

½ pound pitted sour (or sweet) prunes or ¾ pound unpitted

1 tablespoon red wine vinegar

2 tablespoons water

Mix the herbs, cayenne, salt, and garlic in a small bowl with the back of a spoon, pressing against the bowl to mash the herbs and garlic (use a mortar and pestle if you have one).

Mash it until it is almost pasty and sticks together on the back of the spoon.

Put the prunes, vinegar, and water in a saucepan. Bring to a boil, *stirring constantly*. Keep stirring and boiling until the mixture becomes liquidy, about 2 to 3 minutes.

Remove from heat and push through a sieve with a wooden spoon, letting contents fall into a small bowl. Add the mashed herbs and mix thoroughly.

The sauce is complete. It can be refrigerated until needed. When ready to be served, put in a bowl and serve it cold with the *shashlyk*. It may need thinning: To thin the sauce to ketchup consistency, add red wine vinegar a tablespoon at a time, and/or some water. Whether you use more water or vinegar depends upon how sharp you want the sauce to be.

SKEWERED BEEF
(*Basturma*)

Basturma is prepared just like *shashlyk* except that the marinade is different and the meat is broiled without any onions or other vegetables.

(4 TO 6 SERVINGS)

Marinade:

- 1 *onion, sliced*
- 2 *tablespoons fresh, chopped basil or 1 tablespoon crumbled dried basil*
- 1 *tablespoon salt*
- ½ *teaspoon ground black pepper*
- 1 *cup red wine vinegar (or pomegranate juice if you can find some)*

Meat:

2 *pounds beef fillet or sirloin (Cut into cubes, a cheap, tough cut of steak becomes amazingly tender, so if you are feeling poor, don't bother with fancy sirloin.)*

Follow the *shashlyk* instructions, ignoring the lemon, *tkemaly* sauce, and onions.

CHICKEN SALAD OLIVIER
(*Salat Olivier*)

Olivier was the chef of a Russian count. One evening, the story goes, the count had a surprise guest. Since his guest hadn't had any dinner, the count ran into the kitchen and asked his chef, Olivier, to whip something up for dinner. Olivier did not have enough of any part of that evening's dinner to make a respectable-looking platter for the count's guest. So he took some of the leftover game and vegetables, cut everything into cubes, and tossed it with some salad dressing. So, *salat* Olivier is actually a glorified chicken salad.

For the meat, I suggest you use a roasted chicken or turkey, or parts thereof (no point in roasting a bird for this occasion—use leftovers). Remove the meat from the bone and cut it into cubes, as for chicken salad.

For the vegetables, use cooked carrots, peas, potatoes, cooked cucumber, string beans, corn, zucchini . . . almost anything. Just be sure to cook all of them or none of them, so the eaters don't swallow a nice crisp carrot with a mushy potato. Cut all vegetables, when possible, into cubes, the same size as the chicken.

It is also nice to add nuts and apples—but that is not Russian.

Toss the chicken salad with a dressing made with equal parts sour cream and mayonnaise, and some lemon juice, salt, pepper, and chopped fresh coriander. (Don't substitute dill for the coriander; it tastes ridiculous in this salad.)

SEMOLINA, NUT, AND FRUIT PUDDING
(*Gurievskaya Kasha*)

Gurievskaya kasha is called "la pièce de résistance" of Russian desserts. It's a sweet semolina pudding with fruits and nuts—very rich, but there's never any left over. It can be served plain or with cream, grenadine syrup, or a fruit sauce (a thin *kissel*) poured over it. I don't think a sauce is necessary but some Russians do.

NOTES:

This can be made in advance because it has to be served cool anyway. Use milk skins or jam to separate the layers of semolina from the fruit. I have found it impossible to make milk skins so this recipe shows how to make the Kasha with jam. I suspect that part of the difficulty I have found in making milk skins is because American milk is pasteurized and the original recipes for *gurievskaya kasha* were written before pasteurization was made standard.

(8 TO 10 SERVINGS)

2 cups milk

2 cups heavy cream

½ cup sugar

¾ cup semolina or farina

1 cup chopped walnuts or pecans

1 cup chopped blanched almonds

1 cup chopped assorted dried fruits

½ teaspoon almond extract

Butter

10 ounces sieved apricot jam or milk skins

1 cup sliced, peeled, pitless, seedless fresh fruit, such as peaches, pears, apricots . . .

½ cup crumbled zwieback or vanilla cookies

Bring the milk, cream, and sugar to a boil in a saucepan. Add the semolina or farina. Stir constantly over a low flame until mixture thickens (5 minutes). Remove from heat. Allow to cool for 10 minutes.

Add the nuts, dried fruits, and almond extract to the cooled mixture and combine thoroughly, using a spoon.

Grease an 8-inch spring-form pan with butter.

Put one third of the semolina or farina mixture on the bottom of the spring-form pan.

Put a thin layer of apricot jam (about half of it) over the layer of semolina or farina mixture (by the way, the cereal mixture is called *kasha*); or put a milk skin over the *kasha*.

Put half the sliced fresh fruits over the jam—a very thin layer.

Place another third of the *kasha* over the fruit. Spread the remaining jam or the last milk skin over the *kasha*; follow with a second, final, thin layer of fresh fruit; and cover the fruit with the last third of the *kasha*. Smooth out the top nicely with a rubber spatula.

Sprinkle the top with the *very finely* crumbled zwieback or vanilla cookies.

Bake at 350° F. for 30 minutes. Let it cool, then refrigerate. When ready to serve, remove the spring-form pan and cut the dessert into wedges.

RUSSIAN TEA ROOM
VEGETABLE BORSCHT
(*Ovoshny Borscht*)

This version of *borscht* is a vegetarian soup. It is the kind served during the Lenten fast, when no meat can be eaten, and is the verson of *borscht* most people are familiar with—a deep-red broth with julienne-cut beets and cucumbers and a dollop of cold sour cream floating on top.

Borscht is traditionally served with little open-faced tarts filled with cheese—*vatrooshky*. (See pages 30–37, for the meat version of *borscht*.)

(6 SERVINGS)

2 *medium onions*	*Sugar*
2 *small pieces fresh parsley*	*Salt*
2 *small carrots*	2 *eggs, beaten*
½ *bunch celery*	1 *pint sour cream*
1½ *quarts water*	1 *small can diced beets, with*
1 *bunch fresh beets, peeled*	*liquid*
and diced	2 *cucumbers, peeled, seeded,*
½ *teaspoon sour salt*	*and julienned*

GARNISH: *chopped fresh dill*

Clean and finely grind the onions, parsley, carrots, and celery. Put in a kettle with the water, stir, and bring to a boil.

Let boil for 15 minutes. Then add the diced fresh beets and boil for 10 minutes; add sour salt, sugar, and salt to taste. Strain while hot; then let the soup cool a while. When cooled, add the beaten eggs, 1 pint of sour cream, the canned beets, with their liquid, and the cucumbers julienne.

Add more sour cream if desired when serving. Garnish with chopped dill.

NOTE:

Sour salt is concentrated citric acid crystals, sometimes still sold in old-fashioned Jewish delicatessens. If none is available, substitute the juice of one juicy lemon.

KASHA

Kasha is often attributed to Jewish cooking, but it is really of Russian origin. I am giving you the recipe for plain *kasha*, but there are many variations. You can add cooked bow tie noodles, or chopped, sautéed onions, or sliced, sautéed mushrooms, or a combination of all of them. It is also fine plain. Russians like their *kasha* dry, but if you prefer it moist just add more stock or water to the recipe.

Kasha can be used as a vegetable course, or as a stuffing for *pelmeny*.

(4 TO 6 SERVINGS)

1 *cup buckwheat groats*
1 *egg, beaten*
¼ *cup butter*
1 *to 2 cups water or chicken stock*
1 *teaspoon salt (only if you use water instead of stock)*

In a very hot frying pan, toast the groats, tossing them from time to time. When they are very hot and toasted . . .

. . . add the egg and mix so that all the groats are coated with egg.

Mix the butter with the groats, and when it has melted . . .

. . . add the 1 to 2 cups of stock or water and salt, and combine with a fork.

Bring to a boil. Then cover the pot and simmer for 15 minutes.

FRUIT PURÉE
(*Kissel*)

Kissel is a fruit purée, thickened slightly with potato flour. It is called *kissel* because it was originally made out of *"kissel berries,"* meaning "sour berries," also called Cornelian cherries. Their American counterpart is Morello cherry (sour cherries), although cranberries and loganberries are often substituted.

Kissel is now made with any fruit purée; Irina uses any type of fruit in almost any combination. For example, she made us a peach, pear, and apple *kissel*. I prefer the berry *kissels*, and so my recipe has been worked out for strawberry, blueberry, or raspberry *kissels*. Other fruits don't make flavorful puddings unless you just make a straight apple or pear sauce—and if that's the case, you might as well buy baby food.

Some people say you can use cornstarch instead of potato starch to thicken the *kissel*. Irina says only potato starch can be used—and I agree thoroughly. Cornstarch overthickens, and makes the pudding tasteless and gluey. One and a half teaspoons of potato starch is just the right amount of starch for two cups of fruit purée.

Kissel can be served as a dessert soup, with a dollop of sour cream in each bowl, or as a topping for ice cream (in Russia, you will never have a chocolate or fudge sauce on ice cream— *kissel* or some kind of fruit jam is the sauce).

The following is an excerpt from *Vagabond in the Caucasus*, where the vagabond is describing a marketplace:

> . . . At the corner by the bridge there was a huge pile of bright red berries . . . These were cranberries; they can be stewed into a fine-looking pudding. Kissel: sour jelly, they call it; it is bright crimson and looks too good to eat.

(4 TO 6 SERVINGS)

> 2 *cups water*
> 1 *pint blue-, straw-, or raspberries*
> 1 *lemon, thinly sliced*
> 1 *cinnamon stick*
>   *Potato starch*
> 3 *to 6 tablespoons sugar (to taste)*

GARNISH: *sour cream*

Combine the water, berries, lemon, and cinnamon stick in a deep saucepan.

Bring the pot to a boil, lower the heat, and simmer for about ½ hour. Then let the mixture cool.

When cool, remove the cinnamon stick and the lemon, and purée the berries in a food mill or in a blender. Measure the purée.

Return all but ½ cup of the purée to the saucepan.

Take 1½ teaspoons potato starch for every 2 cups of purée. Put the appropriate amount of starch into the ½ cup of purée. Combine the two thoroughly until the starch is dissolved and not lumpy.

Put a low flame under the main pot of purée, and gradually add the ½ cup of starch and purée to the pot while stirring the main purée with a wire whisk. Gradually add the sugar, tasting.

Keep stirring the pudding until it comes to a boil.

When boiling, and the sugar is dissolved, remove from the flame and pour into a serving bowl.

Sprinkle 1 tablespoon of sugar over the top of the pudding (this keeps it from forming a skin on top), then cover with plastic wrap or aluminum foil, and refrigerate.

Serve cold as a pudding with sour cream, or as a topping for ice cream.

VODKA AND ZAKOOSKY

The Russian word meaning "appetizers," *zakoosky,* is derived from the verb *zakooseet,* meaning "to bite." *Zakoosky* are little bites to eat and very similar to the Scandinavian smorgasbord. It is said that *zakoosky* were introduced to Russian cuisine in 862 A.D., when the Scandinavian prince Rurik became the first Czar of Russia.

In Russia, unlimited quantities and varieties of *zakoosky* are served on a large table or sideboard before the main meal of the day. The marinated vegetables, fresh vegetable salads, the meat, the smoked or marinated fish, the caviar, the meat-and vegetable-stuffed pastries (*piroshky*), the little meatballs (*bitky*) are all laid out in separate oval serving dishes. The visual appeal does not rely on elaborate decoration of the *zakoosky*; in fact, as a rule they are virtually undecorated—the variety of colors and textures of the actual ingredients make the *zakoosky* attractive. Besides the plates of *zakoosky* there are baskets of different homemade breads cut into thin cracker-sized slices, and dishes of scalloped curls of butter.

Vodka is also served in almost unlimited varieties and quantities and is a "must" when serving *zakoosky*. Vodka can be flavored with lemon peel, cherry pits, pepper, spices, and herbs.

For a dinner party, there is no need to be as extravagant as Russians in the quantity and variety of *zakoosky* and vodka served. Remember that Russian appetites are extraordinarily large. In general, one or two different *zakoosky* are sufficient and likewise for the vodkas. As a Russian himself tells it, in *Vagabond in the Caucasus* by Stephen Graham, non-Russians just don't have the strength and physical stamina that Russians have.

"There was an Englishman took a glass of Siberian vodka and for two days he was drunk. On the third day he drank a glass of water and that made him drunk again."

When I was doing my Religion homework the other day, I came across the following statement, which confirms the popular belief that Russians are unusually heavy drinkers:

It is reported that an early Russian Czar, faced with the prospect of throwing his weight toward Christianity, Islam or Buddhism, rejected the latter two because both included this proscription:

Do Not Drink Intoxicants.

HUSTON SMITH, *The Religions of Man*

And now allow the secretary, from Chekhov's story "The Siren," to give you a few pointers on how to partake of Russian vodka and *zakoosky*:

"As you enter your house the table should be already set, so that you can sit down at once, stuff your napkin back of your tie and slowly, without haste, stretch your hand for the vodka decanter. You don't pour it into an ordinary vodka glass, but into the small silver glass your grandfather used, and you don't tip it over all at once, but first you heave a sigh, then you rub your hands, lift indifferent eyes to the ceiling and only then, mind you, without any hurry, you raise the glass to your lips and . . . immediately sparks run all over your body . . . " The secretary's face expressed perfect bliss.

"Sparks," he repeated, screwing up his face, "and as soon as you have drunk your vodka, you eat an appetizer . . ."

VODKA

To flavor vodka, let the flavoring agent soak in the specified amount of vodka for the amount of time suggested, or longer if you prefer.

LEMON VODKA *Limmonaya Vodka*

Peel one whole lemon and put the peel in 1 pint of vodka for 4 hours.

CHERRY PIT VODKA   *Vishnyovka Vodka*

Take 20 cherry pits and crack them open (smash them if possible) with a hammer. Soak in 1 pint of vodka for 2 hours.

PEPPER VODKA   *Tertsovka*

Soak 2 teaspoons of peppercorns in 1 pint of vodka for 2 hours.

ANISE VODKA   *Anisovaya Vodka*

Soak 1 tablespoon of anise seeds in 1 pint of vodka for 3 hours.

HERB VODKA   *Travnik*

Put in 1 tablespoon of herbs of your choice and let them soak in 1 pint of vodka for 3 hours.

BUFFALO GRASS VODKA   *Zubrovka*

A Russian is reputed to have bought a broom in America and, upon recognizing the scent of buffalo grass, cut up the broom's bristles and made this delicately flavored vodka.

Take 7 blades of buffalo grass (if you can find it) and put it in 1 pint of vodka. Cover and let stand for 4 hours. Remove all the grass except for one blade.

TEA VODKA   *Chai Vodka*

Let 1 tea bag soak in 1 pint of vodka for 2 hours. Try fancy teas to make it more interesting.

EGGPLANT CAVIAR
(*Baklajannaya Ikra*)

This "poor man's caviar" is a delicious vegetarian summer *zakooska*. Its name is a reference to the eggplant seeds, which look like caviar to one with a creative imagination. It is served in a small bowl accompanied by thin slices of black bread and unsalted butter. The Caucasian variation uses 4 chopped onions and 1 cup minced green pepper. I like this non-Caucasian version better.

(6 SERVINGS)

1 *2-pound eggplant*
1 *medium onion (1 cup),*
    chopped fine
2 *small cloves of garlic (1 tea-*
    spoon), minced
½ *cup minced green pepper*

6 *tablespoons olive oil*
¼ *cup tomato paste or purée,*
    or 2 fresh tomatoes,
    peeled and chopped
1 *teaspoon lemon juice*
    Salt and pepper

Bake the eggplant in a 400° F. oven for about an hour—until the skin is charred and wrinkled.

Meanwhile, chop the onion, garlic, and green pepper. Sauté the onions in 3 tablespoons of the olive oil until they are soft and yellow—not browned! Stir often.

Add the garlic and green pepper and keep cooking, and stirring, until the pepper is soft and tender. Remove the pan from the heat.

When the eggplant's skin is charred, remove from the oven, let it cool so you can handle it, and peel it. The skin should come off easily.

Chop the eggplant fine and add it to the frying pan with

the onion and pepper. Then add the tomato paste, purée, or whatever.

Add 3 more tablespoons of olive oil, replace pan over heat, and thoroughly combine the ingredients by stirring while they cook. Cook until the mixture is very thick, stirring constantly (or often) for 15 to 20 minutes so it doesn't burn. Then stir in the teaspoon of lemon juice and season with salt and pepper.

Serve with black bread and unsalted butter.

This can be made in advance; it keeps well in the refrigerator—up to a week.

CAUCASIAN CHEESE SPREAD
(*Kavkazee Myakee Seer*)

I got this recipe from the chef at the Kavkaz Hotel in Sochi (a resort near the Black Sea). This cheese spread was served as an appetizer at lunch (that's the big meal of the day) with black and white breads.

The recipe calls for Dutch cheese: I have used Fynbo for the cheese, and it is perfect. Any of those round cheeses in red wax seem to do the job.

(4 TO 6 SERVINGS)

7 ounces Dutch cheese
3 ounces walnuts
1 tablespoon butter
12 small cloves or 4 teaspoons finely chopped garlic
  Salt
  Chopped fresh coriander (cilantro) or parsley

Grate the cheese, or put small pieces of it in a blender.

Pulverize the nuts in a grinder, a mortar and pestle, or a blender.

Cream together the cheese, nuts, and butter in a bowl.

Peel the garlic; then smash it with the flat side of a knife. Sprinkle the smashed cloves of garlic with salt and then start chopping. Mince until very fine—almost pulverized.

Mix the garlic and some chopped coriander leaves (about 1 tablespoon) with the cheese. Keep beating the cheese until it is as smooth as possible.

Put the cheese mixture into a ceramic crock or, actually, any kind of wide-mouthed jar—even a bowl will do. Cover and refrigerate until needed. Serve at room temperature.

SALADS WITH SOUR CREAM DRESSING

The sour cream dressing:

> ½ cup sour cream
> ¼ teaspoon lemon juice
> Sugar, salt, and pepper to taste

RADISHES WITH SOUR CREAM

(4 TO 6 SERVINGS)

> 2 bunches radishes
> ½ cup sour cream dressing

Wash and dry the radishes; discard the leaves. Slice thin and place in a shallow dish. Sprinkle with salt, and let stand for ½ hour. Drain in a colander or sieve and put in a bowl. Mix with the sour cream dressing. Chill. Serve. Eat.

WHITE AND RED RADISH SALAD

(4 TO 6 SERVINGS)

 1 *bunch white radishes*
 1 *bunch red radishes*
 ½ *cup sour cream dressing*
 2 *teaspoons Dijon-style mustard*

Peel and grate the white radishes. Wash and grate the red radishes. Combine the grated radishes and toss with sour cream dressing spiced up with mustard.

Chill. Taste before serving to make sure it is highly seasoned. Serve. Eat.

ESTONIAN CUCUMBER SALAD

(4 TO 6 SERVINGS)

 2 *cucumbers*
 Salt
 ¼ *cup sour cream dressing or caraway seeds*

This salad is served either with sour cream dressing or just with caraway seeds sprinkled on top.

Peel the cucumbers and slice paper thin. Put a layer in a dish, sprinkle lightly with salt. Repeat with another layer, some more salt, until you run out of cucumber.

Let the cucumbers stand for 1 to 3 hours. Then squeeze them to get rid of the juice. (Use your imagination to figure out how to squeeze them—if necessary, use your hands; nobody will know what you did to the salad!)

Toss the salad with sour cream dressing or just sprinkle on caraway seeds.

PORK IN ASPIC
(*Kholodyets or Studen*)

(FROM ANNA MARKIEVICH)

This is a classic Russian *zakoosky*. It is composed of pieces of pork in natural gelatin. This can be made very attractive by creating designs with carrots and pimento slices under the gelatin before it hardens. It is served cold with vinegar on the side.

Please don't be upset when you see that the ingredients list includes pigs' feet. I thought it was pretty disgusting also, but it really isn't so bad. If you're terribly squeamish, ask your butcher to chop up the feet so that you won't recognize them.

NOTES:

1. I give instructions for making this dish in an attractive and somewhat refined way. Many Russians, however, will just strain the stock and pour it into a bowl. Then they will cut up the meat, if they use any (poor Russians would just scrape the bits of meat off the feet; this is a high-protein, economical dish), and throw it in the bowl with the broth. Then they'd refrigerate that.

2. The Jews make a similar dish, called *pechad*, out of calves' feet.

(4 TO 6 SERVINGS)

4 pigs' feet
1 pound fresh pork butt
2 bay leaves
10 black peppercorns
4 large cloves garlic
½ teaspoon whole mustard
    seeds

Salt to taste
A carrot or two, cooked, for
    decoration
A small jar of pimentos, or
    roasted peppers

GARNISH: chopped fresh dill and your favorite salad vinegar

Put the pigs' feet, pork butt, bay leaves, peppercorns, garlic, mustard seeds and salt in a pot large enough to hold all of this comfortably—with about 3 inches extra pot height.

Fill the pot with water to cover the meat by an inch. Simmer, uncovered, for about 3 to 4 hours, or until the broth has reduced to the point of just meeting the meat.

Remove the pork butt and put it on a carving board to cool. Throw out the pigs' feet and strain the broth.

Take a rectangular dish or pan about 7 inches wide, 9 inches long, 2 inches deep, and pour just enough of the strained broth to cover the bottom of the pan. Refrigerate immediately. Leave the rest of the strained broth near the stove, so that it doesn't jell before you're ready.

Now, slice the pork butt into thin slices, or into small chunks. Slice the cooked carrot, and cut up the pimentos or roast peppers.

Take a look at the dish with the bit of broth that's in the refrigerator, and if it has jelled, or begun to jell, take it out of the fridge. Place the cooked carrot and pimentos or peppers in a nice design on top of the hardening gelatin. Now carefully pour a little bit more of the strained stock over the design. Refrigerate again, until that layer of stock jells.

Now put all the slices of meat on top of the carrot and pimento design, packing the meat as close together as possible. Pour the remaining broth over the meat, and if it doesn't cover the meat, add a little water until it does. Refrigerate until the broth completely hardens.

When ready to serve, unmold (slip a spatula around the edges of the gelatin, and then invert the dish over a serving plate) and serve garnished with chopped fresh dill. Pass around a bowl of vinegar, to dip the meat slices in.

STUFFED CABBAGE
(*Golubtsy*)

Here's another one of Anna Markievich's recipes, and it is, of course, superb. *Golubtsy* is the Russian version of stuffed cabbage. It is a savory dish, in contrast to the Jewish version with raisins and a sweet and sour sauce. They are excellent as appetizers or as the main course for lunch. Each cabbage leaf is wrapped around a pork, beef, veal, and rice filling. Estonians are known for using three kinds of meat together, so this recipe *may* come from Estonia, but I'm not sure.

In Russian, *golubtsy* means little pigeons. These fat little cabbage rolls are supposed to approximate the shape of pigeons. They really look more like little pillows to me.

(36 CABBAGE ROLLS)

1 *very large head of cab-bage, with dark-green leaves (3 pounds)*	*Salt*
	Butter
	2 *onions, chopped*
	2 *cloves garlic, chopped*

2 pounds pork, beef, veal,
  ground twice (⅔
  pound each type of
  meat)
1 tablespoon chopped
  fresh parsley
1 tablespoon chopped
  fresh dill
  Pepper to taste (use a
  lot of pepper; this is
  supposed to be a
  spicy dish)
1 raw egg
2 cups cooked rice, al
  dente

½ cup water
3 or 4 slices bacon
1 sour salt crystal or the
  juice of 3 juicy
  lemons
2 cups or 16 ounces to-
  mato sauce
2 cups beef stock
2 bay leaves
2 or 3 cloves
½ teaspoon whole allspice
3 tablespoons bacon fat
3 tablespoons flour

NOTES:

1. How to cook rice *al dente*: Take ½ cup of raw rice and follow the normal instructions for cooking rice, only cook it for about half the suggested time, so that the rice is slightly crunchy, or resistant to the teeth.

2. While the *golubtsy* are baking, shake the pan every ½ hour when you go to baste it, so that the cabbage rolls don't stick to the bottom of the pan.

3. Cooked *golubtsy* freeze very well, in case you get frightened by the extraordinary yield of this recipe.

4. It is important to have the casserole *completely* filled with cabbage rolls—otherwise they won't cook well.

Preparations:

Take a good sharp knife, and core the cabbage. That is, run the knife around the round white part of the cabbage that's on the bottom. Then remove that cylinder, or cone-shaped piece of core.

Choose a pot that will hold your whole cabbage snugly with about 4 inches extra. Fill it a half to two thirds full of water and add 1 tablespoon of salt. Bring to a boil.

Put the cored cabbage into the pot of boiling water, bottom-side of the cabbage down. The water should just cover the cabbage. If it doesn't, add some hot tap water to the pot until the cabbage is immersed. As mentioned above, the pot must fit the cabbage snugly or the cabbage will float and you'll never cover it with water! Let the cabbage sit in the hot water, covered but off the flame, for at least 1 hour.

While you are waiting for the cabbage to soften up, sauté in butter 2 chopped onions with 2 chopped cloves of garlic, until onions are translucent, *not* brown.

Now mix the three kinds of meat thoroughly. Add the onions and garlic, the parsley, dill, salt, and pepper to the meat. Mix it all up. Now add the raw egg, and mix again thoroughly.

Now add the 2 cups of cooked rice, *al dente* (see notes), and ½ cup of water. Mix again.

Take the other 2 chopped onions and sauté them with about 3 to 4 slices of bacon (no butter needs to be added to the pan), until the bacon is crisp and before the onions burn.

Remove and set aside the bacon slices. Pour off the excess bacon fat from the onions and put that aside. Now put the sautéed onions on the bottom of a 5-quart casserole.

Cover the sautéed onions with 2 or 3 of the outermost cabbage leaves—as many as needed to line the bottom of the pan.

Now you are ready to make the little pigeons.

Golubtsy

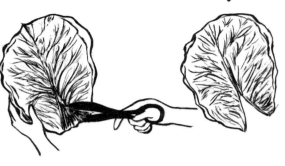

cutting, stuffing and rolling the cabbage

Making the golubtsy:

Take a leaf off the cabbage.

Cut the big vein at the bottom of the leaf, so that it has a triangle chopped out of the base of the leaf.

Place 1 to 1½ tablespoons of meat filling near the point of the missing triangle. The leaf curves here like a shell, so it will be like putting a baby in a cradle.

Now roll the cabbage up around the filling like rolling a cigarette, and then stuff the excess cabbage at the ends of each roll into itself.

Place the cabbage roll in the casserole lined with cabbage leaves.

Repeat this process until you either run out of cabbage leaves, meat, or room in the casserole. Be sure to pack the cabbage tightly but not too tightly, because they need room to expand during cooking. Make only one layer of *golubtsky*, although you will probably make more than one row. The entire pan must be filled with cabbage rolls or else they will open up during cooking and you will have a delicious but unattractive mess.

When you have filled up the pan of cabbages, dissolve the sour salt crystal in the tomato sauce or mix the lemon juice with the beef stock, and then pour this mixture over the cabbage. If the liquids don't cover the pigeons, add more water or stock until they just cover the tops of the cabbage rolls.

Take a piece of cheesecloth, and wrap it around the bay leaves, cloves, and allspice. Tie it with a piece of string so that you have a little spice bag. Put this bag in the center of the casserole.

Cover the casserole with a cover if you have one, or with aluminum foil.

Bake the pigeons for 2 hours at 375° F., basting occasionally with the pan juices (every ½ hour or so). Give the pan a little shake while you're there to keep the cabbage from sticking to the bottom of the pan and burning.

After the pigeons have been cooking almost 2 hours, make a *soprashka*, or what is known in French as a roux. This means heat 3 tablespoons of bacon fat with 3 tablespoons of flour, and brown the flour, mixing constantly with a whisk or wooden spoon. When the flour is a delicately colored brown, add 1 cup of liquid from the casserole of cabbage rolls to the *soprashka*, and mix thoroughly, taking care not let it all get lumpy.

Pour the diluted *soprashka* over the pigeons.

Crumble up the bacon you saved from browning the onions and sprinkle it over the pigeons.

Bake, uncovered, for about 10 to 15 minutes, basting or adding liquid if the cabbage rolls seem dry.

Transfer to a serving.dish with 2-inch high walls.

Serve 1 or 2 per person as an appetizer or 3 or 4 as a lunch, depending upon the delicacy of the eater.

SAVORY STUFFED PIES
Piroshky

A *pirojok* (singular of *piroshky*) is a small finger-shaped pastry enclosing a meat, fish, vegetable or even a sweet cheese or fruit filling. It is a baby *pirog* (A *kulebyaka* is a *pirog*): *pirojok* being the diminutive form of *pirog*. *Piroshky* are often served as a luncheon dish with a bowl of soup. In this case they are about 3 inches long and 2 inches wide in the middle, tapering off at the ends. Made to smaller proportions, so that they are bite-size, *piroshky* are served as *zakoosky*.

There are three basic doughs used for *piroshky* pastry. The classic Russian dough is a sour cream dough. It is simple to make, refrigerates well, and tastes good. A somewhat less simple dough is the raised dough. A *brioche* dough recipe is given here, because it is a good yeast dough for the purpose. The fanciest dough is the puff-pastry dough.

The filling recipes I provide are the most basic, but there are millions of others. Almost anything can be used to fill a *pirojok*. *Piroshky* are perhaps the result of the numerous famines in Russian history. Chopped leftover meat, vegetables, or buckwheat can all be made into a satisfying and delicious meal by using them to fill a piece of dough. This can also explain the use of three or four fillings in a large *pirog*. Now it is made because it tastes good, but it may have originated from having too little of any one food to fill a *pirog*.

The Boyars, a Russian aristocratic order (a notch below princes) abolished by Peter the Great in the eighteenth century, were great fans of *piroshky*. I don't think anyone can blame them.

The most popular *piroshky* shape is the oval shape. It can be made with either yeast or sour-cream dough. If made with an aperture at the top, oval-shaped *piroshky* are called *rass-tyeg-eye*, traditionally made with sour cream dough and a filling of sturgeon and other fish, hard-boiled eggs, and mushrooms. The *kulebyaka* filling (page 94) is a good substitute.

Half-moon-shaped *piroshky*, called *poloomyesyats*, are best made with sour-cream dough.

Triangular-shaped *piroshky* are a good shape for puff-pastry dough. Square-shaped *piroshky* are best made with sour-cream dough. Both triangular and square are called *treoogolnik piroshky*.

IRINA STYEPANOVNA'S DOUGH

This is the authentic yeast dough used for *piroshky*. Much to my dismay, I discovered that it was not only the authentic yeast dough, but also the only dough used for *piroshky* in

Russia. In all the *piroshky* shops, in all the bakeries and snack bars, this was the dough used. Nevertheless, puff-pastry, *brioche*, and sour cream doughs also do the job. One full batch of dough yields about 3 dozen pastries.

1 *package dry yeast or*	1½ *cups milk*
½ *ounce*	4½ to 5 *cups flour*
compressed yeast	1 *teaspoon salt*
¼ *cup lukewarm water*	¼ *cup corn oil*
¼ *cup sugar*	

GLAZE: 1 *egg*
1 *teaspoon milk or cream*

In a bowl sprinkle the yeast over the water and set in an unlit oven to rise. When it foams up and gets all puffy (about 10 minutes), it is ready. Sometimes it helps to feed the yeast a pinch of sugar.

Dissolve the sugar in the milk and stir in the yeast sponge.

Put the flour and salt in a big bowl, and make a well in the center.

Start pouring the yeast mixture into the well, gradually incorporating it with the flour, until you have used up half of it. Then gradually work half the oil into the dough.

Add the rest of the yeast mixture, and then the remaining oil.

The dough should be sticky, although it will be firm enough to stay in a ball when lifted out of the bowl. The kneading process takes place in the bowl, and then you will have a chance to firm up the dough and add ½ to ¾ cup more flour.

Knead the dough in the bowl, incorporating just enough extra flour to make the dough manageable—be stingy. Knead by folding the dough, and then pushing down on it with the heel of your hand.

Periodically, lift the mass of dough out from the bowl, hold the dough way over your head, then slam it down into the bowl. This is Irina's special technique. She says it gets the air out of the dough. You really have to whack it good and hard about 7 or 8 times, and then continue kneading.

The knead–slam process should take about 10 minutes. Give up when the dough feels firm and is smooth, or whenever you get bored.

Oil a bowl lightly, and place the dough in it, turning it over to get all of it coated. Cover with a towel and leave to rise in an unlit oven until double in bulk—1 to 1½ hours.

Assembling the piroshky:

Have the filling all prepared (see pages 223 to 224), the dough risen.

Turn the risen dough out onto a floured board and knead it slightly.

The Russian method will then have you take a golfball-sized hunk of dough from the main mass of dough and cover the main mass with a damp towel to keep it from drying out.

If you are going to be elegant about the business, roll out all the dough, get a giant round cookie cutter of at *least* 4 inches diameter, and stamp out a bunch of circles. (The dough's thickness should be a little less than ¼ inch thick.)

If you use the golfball method, coat the dough with a little flour if it is very sticky, and then shape it into a ball. Flatten the ball into a flat circle, stretching it out so that it is thin. (Russians tend to make the dough very thick but then you don't get in enough filling, and the *pirojok* is mostly dough— so, if necessary, flatten the dough circle with a rolling pin.)

Put 2 tablespoons of filling in the center of the circle, and bring the opposite edges of the circle together, enclosing the

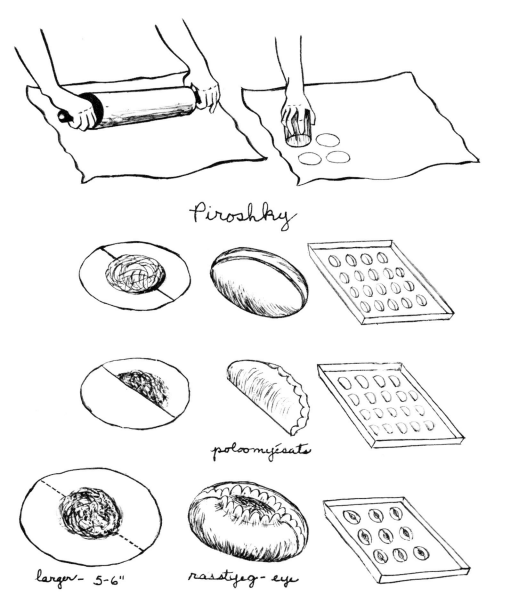

Piroshky

poloomyésats

larger – 5-6"

rasstyeg – eye

filling. Pinch the edges together so that the seam is as smooth as possible. Shape the *pirojok* into a cigar shape, or fat finger, that tapers slightly at each end.

Oil the surface of a large cookie sheet and place the *piroshky* seam side down on the sheet about an inch apart.

Light the oven, and set it at 350° F.

Let the *piroshky* rise for 20 to 30 minutes, while the oven gets hot. Then brush them with a beaten egg mixed with a teaspoon of milk or cream.

Bake until they are a deep golden brown on the top and golden on the sides.

Cool, covered with a damp towel, so that the crust does not harden.

Serve warm.

SOUR CREAM DOUGH

This dough can be used for *piroshky, pirogy, vatrooshky,* and *kulebyaky.* When using it, to keep the *piroshky* from opening up while cooking, brush the inside edges of the dough (before making the seam) with a little bit of beaten egg.

(ABOUT 30 PIROSHKY, APPETIZER SIZE)

3½ *cups sifted flour*
  1 *teaspoon baking powder*
  1 *teaspoon salt*
½ *cup (¼ pound) unsalted*
    butter

2 *eggs, beaten*
1 *cup (or 8 ounces) sour*
  cream

GLAZE: *A beaten egg*

Thoroughly mix the flour, baking powder, and salt in a large bowl.

Add the butter and break it up into small pieces, simultaneously rubbing it in with the flour. Do this until the mixture resembles fine cornmeal or bread crumbs.

In another small bowl mix the eggs and sour cream. Then add them to the flour–butter mixture, and stir. If you don't mind getting your hands a little gloppy, it's probably best to combine the ingredients with your hands.

When the ingredients are well combined, knead the dough on a floured board until it is smooth and pliable (1 to 2 minutes). Form the dough into a ball and lightly coat it with flour.

Chill the dough for at least ½ hour.

Assembling the piroshky:

Roll out the dough to ⅛ inch thickness.

Stamp out circles with a 3-inch cookie cutter if you are making hors d'oeuvres; with a 4-inch to 5-inch cutter if you are making these for lunch. (Russians use different size glasses instead of cookie cutters.)

Brush a circle with beaten egg and then put in the center of each a tablespoon or two of filling, depending on the size of the rounds.

Bring the opposite edges of the circle together and pinch tightly and neatly along the edge. The *piroshky* should be half-moon shaped.

Put the *piroshky* on a metal cookie sheet that has been greased with butter and lightly sprinkled with flour.

Brush the *piroshky* with beaten egg and bake at 400° F. for about 15 minutes, or until golden brown.

BRIOCHE OR RAISED DOUGH

When using a *brioche* dough, the *piroshky* must be cooked seam side down or they will open up when the dough rises.

This *brioche* dough is based on Paula Peck's recipe in *The Art of Fine Baking*.

4 packages dry yeast or 2 ounces fresh yeast	2 teaspoons salt
¾ cup lukewarm milk	1 cup (½ pound) softened unsalted butter
¼ cup sugar	2 egg yolks mixed with 2 teaspoons cream
6 egg yolks and 3 whole eggs	Poppy or caraway seeds (optional)
4 to 5 cups flour	

If dry yeast is used, let it dissolve in the lukewarm milk. If fresh yeast is used, cream it with the sugar to make a syrup, and add lukewarm milk.

Add the egg yolks and eggs to the yeast mixture. Stir well.

Add 3 cups of flour, the 2 teaspoons of salt, and then the softened butter. Knead very well, at least 10 minutes, until the dough is smooth and elastic, adding 1 to 2 cups more flour if necessary to make a medium-firm satiny dough.

Place the dough in a bowl. Dust the top with flour. Cover the bowl with plastic wrap and then with a heavy terrycloth towel and leave in a warm, draft-free place to rise. When it is double in bulk (30 to 40 minutes), punch it down thoroughly. Let the dough rise a second time until it has doubled in bulk again.

If dough is not to be used immediately, refrigerate until it is needed.

Roll out the dough to ⅛-inch thickness on a lightly floured board.

Stamp out circles with a cookie cutter and place a spoonful of filling in the center. Gather the opposite edges of dough together and pinch firmly to enclose the filling.

Mold the *piroshky* in your hand to make a round or oval shape.

Place them on a lightly buttered baking sheet, *pinched side down*. Let them rise until almost double in bulk.

Brush the *piroshky* with 2 egg yolks mixed with 2 teaspoons of cream. Sprinkle with poppy or caraway seeds if you feel like it. Bake at 375° F. for 20 to 30 minutes, or until the rolls are golden brown.

Serve warm.

QUICK PUFF PASTRY

(FROM LIBBY HILLMAN'S LESSONS IN GOURMET COOKING)

This dough is good for both *piroshky* and *kulebyaky*.

(10 TO 20 PASTRIES, DEPENDING ON SIZE)

> 1 *pound unsalted butter, chilled*
> 4 *cups all-purpose white flour, unsifted*
> ½ *teaspoon salt*
> ¾ *cup water*
> ¼ *cup white vinegar*
> 1 *egg*

Flour a pastry cloth or a board.

Place the butter in a large bowl. Add the flour and salt. Using one hand for working, blend the butter and flour together for 30 seconds, breaking butter into large lumps.

Make a well, add the water, vinegar, and egg. Stir wet ingredients and gradually blend in the butter and flour. Combine all very lightly with your hand for 1 minute. The mixture will be uneven, lumpy, and somewhat unmixed. Turn it onto cloth or board.

Roll the mixture back and forth with rolling pin to as near an oblong shape as possible. This first rolling will appear somewhat messy, yet dough will begin to take shape. Scoop up any loose bits of butter or flour and place them on the center of the dough.

Fold by placing the top third over the center third. Then fold the bottom third over center. You now have 3 layers of dough. As in closing a book, fold the dough in half from right to left. You now have 6 layers.

At this point, turn the dough around once to the left. Now roll dough again into a long, thick (½-inch) strip.

Repeat folding and turning as above 4 times, or until dough is solid and somewhat elastic. If, during the rolling-out process, the dough becomes sticky, refrigerate it for 30 minutes and then continue the same rolling and folding.

Cover dough well and refrigerate overnight before using. This dough may be kept up to 3 weeks in your refrigerator.

Baking directions:

Preheat the oven to 425° F.

Shape the *piroshky* into crescents or triangles, being sure to glue the edges together with beaten egg yolk. With a knife make 2 or 3 slashes in the top of each pastry. Then glaze each with an egg beaten with a teaspoon of milk or cream.

Refrigerate the shaped *piroshky* or *kulebyaky* before baking.

Place *piroshky* or *kulebyaky* on an ungreased jellyroll pan, preferably covered with silicone-treated paper.

Bake at 425° F. for 10 minutes, then lower the temperature to 375° F. for the rest of the cooking time. Do not open the oven door for at least the first 10 minutes of baking.

Piroshky take about 25 minutes' baking time. *Kulebyaky* take about 40 to 50 minutes.

FILLINGS FOR *PIROSHKY, PELMENY, PIROGY, KULEBYAKY*

CARROT FILLING

(FOR 36 SMALL PIROSHKY)

> 1½ *pounds carrots, peeled and grated*
> 1 *small onion, finely chopped*
> 2 *tablespoons butter*
> *Salt, pepper, and dill to taste*
> 2 *hard-boiled eggs, finely chopped*

Prepare the carrots as indicated.

Sauté the chopped onion in the 2 tablespoons of butter. When lightly browned, add the carrots and seasoning. Let cook over low heat, covered, for 7 minutes. Remove from heat and let cool.

Add the chopped eggs, mix and taste for seasoning.

CABBAGE FILLING

(FOR 36 SMALL PIROSHKY)

> 1 *medium onion, finely chopped*
> 2 *tablespoons butter*
> 1 *head cabbage (2 pounds), shredded*
> 2 *hard-boiled eggs, finely chopped*
> *Salt, pepper, and dill to taste*

Sauté the chopped onion in butter. When lightly browned, add the shredded cabbage to the pan and cover it. Simmer for 15 minutes over a low flame. If the cabbage looks too dry, and begins to burn, add a tablespoon of water at a time until the mixture is safe from burning and sticking to the pan.

When the cabbage is tender, remove from the pan and let it cool. When cool, mix in the chopped hard-boiled eggs, the salt and pepper, and the chopped dill.

MEAT FILLING

(FOR 36 SMALL PIROSHKY)

    1 *medium onion, chopped*
    2 *tablespoons butter*
    1 *pound chopped beef*
      Salt, pepper, and dill to taste
      Optional: ¼ to ½ cup cooked rice

Brown the chopped onion in 2 tablespoons of butter.

Add the chopped meat to the onions and cook, stirring occasionally, so that the meat separates into "grains" and gets browned on all sides.

Remove the meat mixture from the pan and season with salt, pepper, and dill to taste. Add some cooked rice to the meat if it appeals to you.

If the meat filling is dry, moisten it with a tablespoon or two of water.

APPLE FILLING

I had dessert *piroshky* filled with jams and ground prunes and apples. I especially liked some apple-filled *piroshky* they served at a tea farm in Sochi. These are attractive whether made as a large pie (*pirog*) or as small *piroshky*.

Follow directions for apple purée (see page 27), only don't purée the cooked apples, leave them sliced.

TYPES OF PIROSHKY

RASSTYEG-EYE

These are large *piroshky* served with a pat of butter in the opening. The traditional filling is made of sturgeon and other fish, hard-boiled eggs, and mushrooms. I would suggest the *kulebyaka* filling without the rice. These should be about 5 or 6 inches long. Use *brioche* or sour cream dough.

POLOOMYESYATS PIROSHKY

These are half-moon-shaped *piroshky*. This is the most common shape, and it is good with sour cream dough.

TREOOGOLNIK PIROSHKY

These are triangular-shaped *piroshky*, and are perfect for puff-pastry *piroshky*. Sour cream dough can be used for both types.

SAVORY DUMPLINGS
(*Pelmeny*)

Pelmeny are dumplings that resemble Jewish *kreplach* and Chinese *won tons* and Italian *ravioli*. They came to Russia from China through the eastern provinces, perhaps as early as the beginning of the Christian era, when trade routes had been established to China. If *pelmeny* didn't enter Russian kitchens then, they surely came with the arrival of Genghis Khan and the Mongol invasion in the thirteenth century.

In far eastern Russia and Siberia, *pelmeny* are made in a

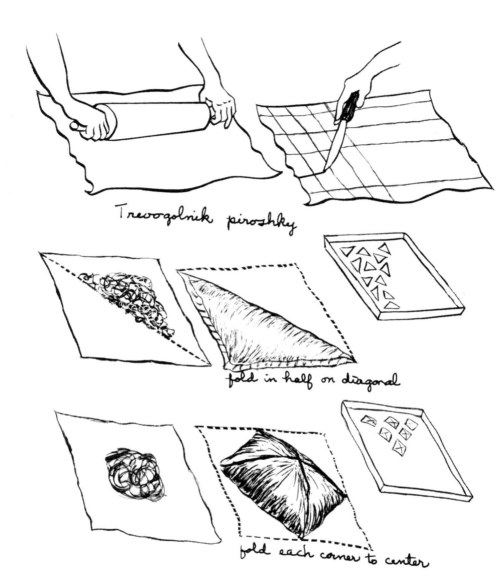

Trevogolnik piroshky

fold in half on diagonal

fold each corner to center

half-moon shape and served with soy sauce, melted butter, vinegar or a sauce of vinegar and mustard. Siberian housewives would make enormous batches of *pelmeny* and keep them outside in the snow. Their husbands would take bags of frozen *pelmeny* on hunting trips. To have a good, fast meal, all they had to do was fill up a pot with snow and heat it, and then boil the *pelmeny* in the melted snow.

Pelmeny, being very small, can make a little bit of meat go a long way, and they were therefore used when there was a shortage of meat; in addition, they were used as a convenient storage method for scraps of meat in anticipation of a future famine. Now the motive for making *pelmeny* is purely desire; it is a vestige of an old culture.

The dough and filling for *pelmeny* are very simple and quick to make. The time-consuming part is filling up little circles of dough with the meat. To quicken the process, forget how cute they look the smaller they are, and keep them a decent size. Don't make them too big or the filling will not cook (that is only important if you use an uncooked meat filling). Also, if they are to be served in soup, bear in mind that they should be bite size and soup-spoon size.

In Russia, there are little *pelmeny* shops for quick snacks. As early as ten o'clock in the morning, people are eating the light meat dumplings in the *pelmeny* shops.

In Moscow, they serve the *pelmeny* with melted butter and sour cream on a plate. You eat standing at chest-high round tables.

In Kiev, *vareniky* shops, the Ukrainian counterpart of the *pelmeny* shops, are popular. These dumplings are very similar to *pelmeny*, the only difference being that *vareniky* have sweet fillings, whereas *pelmeny* usually enclose meat. The lines at the *vareniky* shops are discouragingly long, but it is definitely worth the wait!

NOTES:

1. Follow the method for making the dough exactly. This is how Irina makes them, and it is also the only way to keep them from turning into tough leaden dumplings, better known as sinkers. Anna Markievich describes her own *pelmeny* as being: "Oh, so light! When people come to my house for *pelmeny* or *vareniky—they know, Anna never makes sinkers!*"

(6 SERVINGS)

The dough:

2 *cups flour: all-purpose white for Siberian style; buckwheat for Ukrainian style*
1 *teaspoon salt*
1 *egg, slightly beaten*
⅔ *cup water*

Combine the flour and salt on a board. Mound up the flour, and make a well in the center.

Pour into the well the egg and the water.

Using a soup spoon, start pushing some of the flour from the top edge of the well into the liquid center. Do this in a circular motion, going all around the top of the well. Start combining the flour and liquid as you do this.

When the liquids are absorbed by a minimal amount of flour (the well should still exist, but the mountain, or volcano, is shorter and the center is a gooey dough), start folding in the ring of surrounding flour, *gradually*, with your hand.

Knead or mix the dough slightly, just enough to get the dough together in a coherent mass.

Refrigerate until needed.

The meat filling:

> 1 medium onion, minced
> 1 clove of garlic, minced
> Butter
> 1 pound chopped beef
> Salt and pepper to taste

Sauté the onions and garlic in a frying pan with butter until they are soft but not browned.

Mix the onions with the raw meat and add salt and pepper to taste.

Preparing the Pelmeny:

> Flour
> A glass of cold water
> 3 quarts salted water

Roll half of the dough at a time on a floured board to $\frac{1}{16}$ inch thickness.

With a circular cookie cutter, 2 inches in diameter, cut out circles. (These can also be made in a triangular shape: cut dough into squares and fold over the filling.)

Put 1 teaspoon of filling in the center of a dough circle; cram in as much filling as you can.

Moisten the edge of the dough with cold water. Bring one side of the dough over the filling, to meet the other edge, forming a half-moon-shaped pelmeny. Seal the edge tightly by pinching it.

Bring the salted water to a boil in a big pot. When it is boiling vigorously, drop in a few pelmeny (4 or 5 at a time).

They are ready when they rise to the top and are floating, sort of like dead gold fish in a fish bowl (a minimum of 5 minutes cooking, no matter how soon they float!).

Remove from water with a slotted spoon and let drain in a colander.

Ways to serve pelmeny:

Siberian style:

1. Serve on a platter with a vinegar and mustard sauce poured over them:

> ¼ cup Dijon-style mustard mixed with
> ¼ cup white-wine vinegar

2. Serve on a platter with soy sauce poured over them.
3. Serve on a platter with white-wine vinegar poured over them.

Central Russian style:

1. Serve on a platter with sour cream poured over them.
2. Serve on a platter with melted butter poured over them.
3. Serve in bowls of consommé or bouillon.

NOTE:

Pelmeny may be frozen after they have been boiled. To use frozen *pelmeny*, just throw them in a pot of boiling snow or water.

DESSERT DUMPLINGS
(*Vareniky*)

These dumplings can be made with sweetened cheese filling or fruit or nut filling. They are served with confectioner's sugar and sour cream or melted butter. The fruit and cheese dumplings can also be served with *kissel.*

(6 SERVINGS)

1 *recipe* pelmeny dough *(see page 228)*
1 *pound cheese filling (see page 37), sweetened to taste*
    Or: 1 *batch fruit filling*
    Or: 1 *batch nut filling*
    Or: ½ *batch apple purée (see page 27), but don't purée cooked apples. Leave them sliced.*

Follow the directions for making *pelmeny,* except do not boil in salted water. Leave the water plain.

NUT FILLING

1 *cup finely ground almonds or walnuts*
1 *to 2 tablespoons ground cinnamon*
⅔ *cup honey*

Mix the nuts with the cinnamon—vary the amount of cinnamon according to your taste.

Gradually mix the honey into the nut mixture, a little bit at a time, using more or less honey until the mixture just manages to hold together.

Use about 1 teaspoon of filling per dumpling.

STRAWBERRY FILLING

1 *pint strawberries*
Brown sugar

Clean and hull the strawberries and slice them.

Put some brown sugar in a bowl, and coat the strawberry slices with this sugar.

Fill each dumpling with two slices of strawberry.

RUSSIAN BLACK BREAD
(*Chorny Hlyeb*)

What Russian cookbook would be complete without a recipe for Russian black bread that works?

The secret to Russian black bread is using bread crumbs for some of the flour. What you can do is save all the crusts or stale pieces of bread that naturally accumulate and put them in a blender—or you can go out and buy a loaf of dark bread and let it go stale and then make crumbs. (To quicken the staling process, crumble up the bread and toast it in the oven.) Use these crumbs for the first batch of black bread. Then save the ends or stale pieces of the black bread that you've made and make those into crumbs. Each subsequent loaf will be darker.

Using bread crumbs must have been the invention of a frugal cook, and frugal cooks must have been common in Old Russia, as much of Russian cooking indicates. Russian black bread belongs in the group of "save-it-you-might-need-it-later" foods, along with *piroshky* and apple *sharlotka*.

(2 LOAVES)

2 *cups rye flour*
3+ *cups all-purpose white flour*
2 *cups toasted bread crumbs (preferably black bread crumbs)*
½ *cup bran (Commercial cereal may be used, although it gives a little [nice] sweetness to the bread.)*

¼ *cup unsweetened cocoa*
½ *teaspoon fennel seeds, crushed*
2 *tablespoons caraway seeds*
1 *tablespoon salt*
¼ *teaspoon ground ginger*
⅛ *pound (½ stick) butter*
¼ *cup molasses or dark corn syrup*

2 ounces compressed yeast or
  4 packages dry yeast
1 teaspoon sugar
¼ cup strong coffee or 1 tablespoon instant coffee dissolved in ¼ cup water

2 cups lukewarm water
Cornmeal, poppy seeds, or
  flour

GLAZE: 1 egg yolk
       1 teaspoon water
       1 teaspoon Postum or instant coffee

Preparations:

Combine the rye flour, white flour, crumbs, bran, cocoa, fennel seeds, caraway seeds, salt, and ginger.

Melt the butter and combine it with the molasses. Let the mixture cool to lukewarm. Meanwhile . . . crumble the yeast (if compressed) and mix it with the sugar; if it's dry, just dissolve it with the sugar in the lukewarm molasses-butter mixture. When the compressed yeast has begun to dissolve with the sugar, mix it with the molasses-butter mixture.

Combine the coffee and warm water.

Assembly and baking:

Put half the dry ingredients in a huge mixing bowl.

Add the warm water–coffee mixture and beat with a wooden spoon until combined. Then add the dissolved yeast–molasses mixture, and beat.

Gradually add more dry ingredients (not *all*, about half of what is left). Keep beating. Then, again gradually, add the rest of the dry ingredients until the dough is solid and manageable. It is a moist dough.

Turn the dough out onto a lightly floured board. Knead it

until smooth and firm, adding more flour to the board to keep from making a sticky, gooey mess.

Form the dough into a ball and put it in an oiled bowl. Turn the dough ball over so that both sides are coated with a thin film of oil.

Cover the bowl with plastic wrap and a terrycloth towel and let rise in a warm draft-free place. (An unlit oven works very well.) This rising should take about an hour, maybe more. When the dough mass is double in bulk and when it will keep a dent after you have poked it with your finger, it is ready.

Punch down the dough. Cut it in half.

Knead each half on a lightly floured board just long enough to make the dough firm enough to mold into nice round shapes.

Sprinkle some cornmeal, poppy seeds, or flour on the bottom of a cookie sheet.

Place the dough rounds on the cookie sheet, and with a single-edged razor blade or a sharp knife, slash a cross in the center of each round. Cover with a lightly moistened towel and let rise for ½ hour—or until double in bulk.

Meanwhile, preheat the oven to 375° F.

Bake the bread for 30 minutes and then brush the tops with a glaze: 1 egg yolk mixed with 1 teaspoon of water and 1 teaspoon of Postum or instant coffee.

Continue baking for 10 minutes more and then test to see if the bread is ready: Stick a skewer in the bread; if it comes out clean, the bread is ready. Or lift up the loaf and tap it on the bottom. If it has a nice hollow sound, it is ready.

Let the bread cool on a rack. If you cut bread while it is still very hot, it will be soggy.

Index

Currently a sophomore at Yale College, Jane Blanksteen was born and bred in New York City. Her Russian grandmother approves of this book; so did her teachers at Phillips Exeter Academy, for whom she started it; and her publishers, for whom she finished it.